AGS

English to Use

by
Barbara A. Trautman
David H. Trautman

AGS®
American Guidance Service, Inc.
Circle Pines, Minnesota 55014-1796
800-328-2560

About the Authors

Barbara Ainsworth Trautman has taught English and social studies for more than thirty years at the elementary, secondary, and college levels. In addition, she has taught curriculum and methods courses for several universities. She holds a Ph.D. in curriculum and has served as curriculum coordinator for American overseas schools in the United States, Central America, and Africa. Dr. Trautman has taught English on four continents—most recently in China.

David H. Trautman has been a professional writer of technical materials for industry and instructional materials for education. He holds a Masters degree in education and has taught English, journalism, composition, and math to international students in Central America, Africa, and China.

Photo Credits: p. i—Images ©1996 PhotoDisc, Inc.; p. 2—Dennis MacDonald/PhotoEdit; pp. 26, 130—Tony Freeman/PhotoEdit; p. 48—Patterson Graphics, Inc.; p. 66—Myrleen Ferguson Cate/PhotoEdit; pp. 90, 198—PhotoEdit; pp. 112, 156—Images ©1996 PhotoDisc, Inc.; pp. 178, 218—©Jim Whitmer; p. 260—©Comstock, Inc.

Printed in the United States of America

ISBN 0-7854-1450-9

Product Number 90120

A 0 9 8 7 6 5 4 3 2

Contents

Introduction x

Chapter 1

Building Sentences. 2
Lesson 1   Sentences 4
Lesson 2   Nouns. 6
Lesson 3   Adjectives. 8
Lesson 4   Action Verbs 10
Lesson 5   Adverbs 12
Lesson 6   Adverbs Tell "When". 14
Lesson 7   Adverbs Tell "Where" 16
Lesson 8   Complete and Simple Sentence Parts 18
Lesson 9   Sentence or Fragment? 20
Lesson 10   Writing Mechanics 22
■ Chapter Review 24
■ Test Taking Tip 25

Chapter 2

Adding Prepositions. 26
Lesson 1   Prepositional Phrases 28
Lesson 2   Adjective Prepositional Phrases. 30
Lesson 3   Confusing Subjects 32
Lesson 4   Adverb Prepositional Phrases 34
Lesson 5   Preposition or Adverb?. 36
Lesson 6   Two or More Prepositional Phrases. 38
Lesson 7   Hidden Verbs. 40
Lesson 8   All Kinds of Prepositional Phrases 42
Lesson 9   Writing Mechanics 44
■ Chapter Review 46
■ Test Taking Tip 47

See page 1 to find out more about the sign language shown in this book.

A   B   C   D

Chapter 3

Using Compound Parts 48

Lesson 1   Conjunctions. 50
Lesson 2   Compound Subjects 52
Lesson 3   Compound Predicates 54
Lesson 4   Compounds and Prepositions 56
Lesson 5   Compound Sentences. 58
Lesson 6   Sentences With Compounds 60
Lesson 7   Writing Mechanics 62
■ Chapter Review 64
■ Test Taking Tip 65

Chapter 4

Direct Objects. 66

Lesson 1   What Is a Direct Object?. 68
Lesson 2   Compound Direct Objects. 70
Lesson 3   More Compounds. 72
Lesson 4   Direct Objects and Prepositional Phrases. . . . 74
Lesson 5   Nouns in a Sentence 76
Lesson 6   Pronouns in a Sentence 78
Lesson 7   Using Pronouns. 80
Lesson 8   Pronoun or Adjective? 82
Lesson 9   *This, That; These, Those* 84
Lesson 10   Writing Mechanics 86
■ Chapter Review 88
■ Test Taking Tip 89

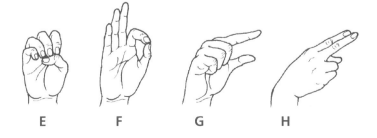

E   F   G   H

Chapter 5	**Practice With Parts of Speech** **90**
	Lesson 1 Assorted Parts of Speech 92
	Lesson 2 Using Owner Words 94
	Lesson 3 Owner Pronouns. 96
	Lesson 4 More Than One Owner 98
	Lesson 5 Hidden Subjects 100
	Lesson 6 More About Adverbs 102
	Lesson 7 Interjections. 104
	Lesson 8 The Writing Process 106
	Lesson 9 Writing Mechanics 108
	■ Chapter Review 110
	■ Test Taking Tip 111

Chapter 6	**More Sentence Patterns** **112**
	Lesson 1 Indirect Objects. 114
	Lesson 2 Indirect Objects in Long Sentences. 116
	Lesson 3 Object Complements 118
	Lesson 4 Object Complements in Long Sentences 120
	Lesson 5 Appositives 122
	Lesson 6 Writing Practice 124
	Lesson 7 Writing Mechanics 126
	■ Chapter Review 128
	■ Test Taking Tip 129

I   J   K   L

Chapter 7

Sentences With Linking Verbs **130**

Lesson 1   Noun Subject Complements 132
Lesson 2   Nouns That Give New Names 134
Lesson 3   Adjective Subject Complements 136
Lesson 4   Adjectives Always Describe Nouns 138
Lesson 5   Adjective or Adverb? 140
Lesson 6   Subject Complements in Long Sentences 142
Lesson 7   Pronouns in Subject Complement Sentences. 144
Lesson 8   More Pronouns 146
Lesson 9   Reviewing Sentence Patterns 148
Lesson 10   Writing Practice 150
Lesson 11   Writing Mechanics 152
■ Chapter Review 154
■ Test Taking Tip 155

Chapter 8

Verbs Tell Time **156**

Lesson 1   Another Look at Verbs 158
Lesson 2   Helping Verbs 160
Lesson 3   The Present Tense 162
Lesson 4   The Past Tense 164
Lesson 5   The Future Tense 166
Lesson 6   Negatives 168
Lesson 7   Verbs That Change Form 170
Lesson 8   Writing Practice 172
Lesson 9   Writing Mechanics 174
■ Chapter Review 176
■ Test Taking Tip 177

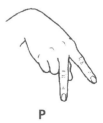

M   N   O   P

Chapter 9

Be Exact **178**
Lesson 1   Writing for Yourself 180
Lesson 2   *Accept, Except; Teach, Learn* 182
Lesson 3   Pronouns or Contractions? 184
Lesson 4   *Lie, Lay; Sit, Set; Rise, Raise* 186
Lesson 5   *To, Too, Two; Let, Leave* 188
Lesson 6   Say *No* Only Once 190
Lesson 7   Writing Practice 192
Lesson 8   Writing Mechanics 194
■ Chapter Review 196
■ Test Taking Tip 197

Chapter 10

Making Sentences Work **198**
Lesson 1   Tone of Voice 200
Lesson 2   What Sentences Can Do 202
Lesson 3   Questions 204
Lesson 4   Compound and Complex Sentences 206
Lesson 5   More About Complex Sentences 208
Lesson 6   Punctuating Quotations 210
Lesson 7   Writing Practice 212
Lesson 8   Writing Mechanics 214
■ Chapter Review 216
■ Test Taking Tip 217

Q   R   S   T

Chapter 11

Writing for Others **218**

Lesson 1   Write the Facts. 220
Lesson 2   Facts Make News. 222
Lesson 3   Writing a Paragraph to Describe 224
Lesson 4   Writing a Process Paragraph 226
Lesson 5   Writing a Paragraph to Persuade 228
Lesson 6   Writing a Story 230
Lesson 7   Writing a Review. 232
Lesson 8   Writing a Letter to a Friend 234
Lesson 9   Writing Mechanics 236
■ Chapter Review 238
■ Test Taking Tip 239

Chapter 12

Spelling. **240**

Lesson 1   Practice Spelling 242
Lesson 2   Homonyms—Words That Sound Alike 244
Lesson 3   More Homonyms 246
Lesson 4   Plurals—Two or More 248
Lesson 5   Other Word Endings. 250
Lesson 6   *Ie or Ei?*. 252
Lesson 7   Words That Look Similar. 254
Lesson 8   Writing Mechanics 256
■ Chapter Review 258
■ Test Taking Tip 259

U   V   W

Chapter 13	**Fine-Tuning Your Writing**	**260**
	Lesson 1 Subject-Verb Agreement	262
	Lesson 2 More About Subject-Verb Agreement.	264
	Lesson 3 Pronoun Subjects With Verb Agreement	266
	Lesson 4 Pronoun-Noun Agreement	268
	Lesson 5 *Don't* and *Doesn't*	270
	Lesson 6 Misplaced Words and Phrases	272
	Lesson 7 Standard English.	274
	Lesson 8 Writing Mechanics	276
	■ Chapter Review	278
	■ Test Taking Tip	279

Glossary **281**

Signing Alphabet **286**

Index **288**

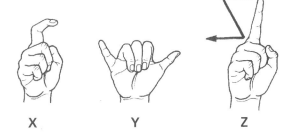

X   Y   Z

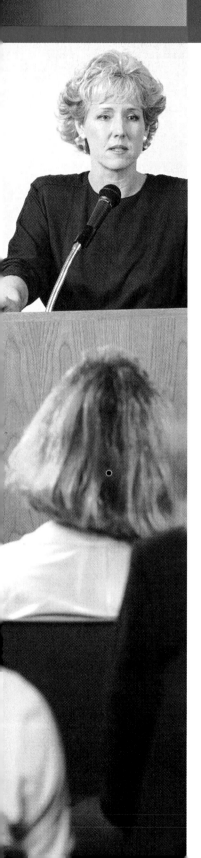

Introduction

When you stand in front of an audience to give a speech, you expect people to pay attention and listen. If you and the people in the audience all speak English, this is a reasonable expectation. You must use the English language correctly, however, if you want your message to be understood.

You use language to communicate whenever you speak or write. The English language is made up of letters and sounds arranged in patterns to form words. Words are arranged in patterns to form sentences. Groups of sentences form paragraphs. Groups of paragraphs form stories, articles, reports, letters, and so on.

Each word in the English language is a part of speech. In this book, you will learn about:

Nouns	Words that name people, places, and things
Pronouns:	Words that take the place of nouns
Verbs:	Words that show action or state-of-being
Adjectives:	Words that describe nouns or pronouns
Adverbs:	Words that tell about verbs, adjectives, or other adverbs
Prepositions:	Words that relate nouns and pronouns to other words in a sentence
Conjunctions:	Words that connect words and ideas
Interjections:	Words that show strong feelings

As you learn about the parts of speech, you will learn how they work in sentences. You will also learn how to arrange the parts of speech to form a variety of sentence patterns. Sentence variety adds interest to any type of writing you do.

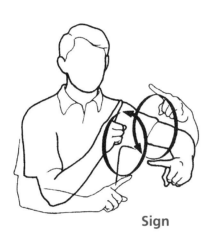

Sign

Communication is important. Hearing people use spoken words to communicate in the English language. Many hearing-impaired people rely on hand signs and gestures to communicate. They use a language called American Sign Language (ASL). Each chapter of this book will help you to communicate better in English. Illustrations in each chapter will show how hearing-impaired people communicate words or a sentence that you are learning in English. Clear communication can connect people with one another both in words and in signs.

Building Sentences

Have you ever watched children build something out of blocks? They put one block on top of another until a house takes shape. Or maybe they build a bridge or a tower. You can build almost anything.

Words are like blocks. When you put words together, you build sentences. Each word in a sentence is important. When words are put together correctly, they form sentences that can be understood.

In this chapter, you will study words as parts of speech. You will also look at how words fit into parts of sentences.

Goals for Learning

▶ To recognize subject | predicate as sentence parts, and subject + verb as a sentence pattern

▶ To identify nouns, adjectives, verbs, and adverbs

▶ To demonstrate the purpose and use of different parts of speech

▶ To distinguish between simple subjects and simple predicates and complete subjects and complete predicates

▶ To tell the difference between a sentence and a fragment

▶ To write complete sentences

Capital letter
A letter that is uppercase. A is a capital or uppercase letter; a is a lowercase letter.

Exclamation point (!)
A punctuation mark showing strong feeling.

Period (.)
The punctuation mark ending a sentence that makes a statement or gives a command.

Predicate
The part of a sentence that tells what the subject is doing.

Question mark (?)
A punctuation mark that ends a sentence asking a question.

Sentence
A group of words that forms a complete thought; a sentence begins with a capital letter and ends with a period, question mark, or exclamation point.

Subject
The part of a sentence that tells who or what the sentence is about.

People speak and write in sentences. A **sentence** is a group of words that tells a complete idea. A sentence has a **subject** and a **predicate**. The subject is the part of a sentence that tells who or what the sentence is about. The predicate is the part of a sentence that tells what the subject is doing.

Every sentence begins with a **capital letter,** or uppercase letter. Every sentence ends with a **period (.),** a **question mark (?),** or an **exclamation point (!).**

EXAMPLE	Sentence:	Ice melts.
	Parts of sentence:	subject | predicate

(*Ice* is the subject of the sentence. *Ice* tells what the sentence is about. *Melts* is the predicate in the sentence. *Melts* tells what the subject is doing.)

Activity A Write these sentences on your paper. Label the subject and predicate in each sentence.

1) People sleep.

2) Cats climb.

3) Tools break.

4) Cars run.

5) Teams play.

Activity B Write a different one-word predicate for each of these subjects. Write the complete sentences on your paper.

1) Boys _____ .

2) Birds _____ .

3) Women _____ .

4) Waves _____ .

5) Wolves_____ .

Activity C Write a different one-word subject for each of these predicates. Write the complete sentences on your paper.

1) _____ grow.

2) _____ sit.

3) _____ sleep.

4) _____ walk.

5) _____ sing.

6) _____ roar.

7) _____ talk.

8) _____ break.

9) _____ play.

Sentence pattern
The basic form of a sentence.

The order of words in a sentence is important. The English language has patterns of word order in sentences. In this lesson, you have been reading and writing the first **sentence pattern**, subject and verb. A sentence pattern is the basic form of a sentence.

EXAMPLE	Sentence:	Ice melts.
	Sentence pattern:	subject + verb

Activity D Copy the sentences. Fill in the blanks on your paper.

1) A sentence has two parts. The two parts are the _____ and the _____ .

2) Read this sentence:

Students write.

Students is the _____ of the sentence, and *write* is the _____ of the sentence.

3) The sentence pattern for *Students write* is:

_____ + _____

Every word in the English language is a part of speech. A **noun** is a part of speech. Nouns are words that name. A noun names a person, a place, or a thing. The subject of a sentence is usually a noun.

Noun

A word that names a person, place, or thing.

EXAMPLES

Sentence:	Truckers drive.
Parts of sentence:	subject	predicate
Sentence pattern:	subject + verb

(*Truckers* is a noun that tells the name of persons.)

Sentence:	Cities grow.
Parts of sentence:	subject	predicate
Sentence pattern:	subject + verb

(*Cities* is a noun that tells the name of places.)

Sentence:	Bells ring.
Parts of sentence:	subject	predicate
Sentence pattern:	subject + verb

(*Bells* is a noun that tells the name of things.)

Activity A Find the nouns in these sentences. Write the nouns on your paper.

1) Salespeople walk.
2) Pilots fly.
3) Kings rule.
4) Leaders plan.
5) Mice squeak.
6) Clowns laugh.
7) Artists paint.
8) Children play.
9) Swimmers float.
10) Students study.

Activity B Find the noun in each group. Write the nouns on your paper.

1) write author sing
2) play govern nation
3) Tom eat walk
4) speak tell street
5) say school come

6) table sit think
7) chew purr kitten
8) buy tape remember
9) find call dog
10) enjoy women talk

Activity C Write each sentence on your paper. Underline the nouns.

1) Fires burn.
2) Trumpets blare.
3) Telephones ring.
4) Trees grow.
5) Winds blow.

6) Lightning strikes.
7) Snow falls.
8) Glass breaks.
9) Flowers droop.
10) Needles hurt.

Activity D Find the nouns in these sentences. Write each noun on your paper. Tell if it names a person, place, or thing.

1) Chains rattle.
2) Pilots fly.
3) Stereos play.
4) Rivers flow.
5) Leaders speak.
6) Doors creak.

Activity E Answer each of these items on your paper.

1) Nouns tell the names of persons, _____ , or _____ .
2) Write the nouns in this list:

house	car	did	flowers
day	driver	streets	teacher
books	person	cloud	town
horse	chairs	tell	sit

3) Write five other nouns.

An **adjective** is a part of speech. Adjectives describe nouns. An adjective gives more information about a noun.

EXAMPLE

Ice cream melts.
| . | | |
adjective noun verb

Parts of speech: adjective noun verb

Parts of sentence: subject | predicate

Sentence pattern: subject + verb

(*Ice* is not a noun in this sentence. *Ice* tells what kind of cream. *Cream* is a noun. *Ice* is an adjective used to describe the noun *cream*.)

Activity A Write each sentence on your paper. Circle the adjectives. Draw a line under the nouns. All these sentences use the subject + verb pattern.

1) Little birds sing.

2) Hungry wolves howl.

3) White clouds float.

4) Big ships sail.

5) Empty cars sit.

6) Happy people laugh.

Nouns can have many adjectives that describe them.

EXAMPLE   **Mean, old, ugly** bears roared.

Activity B Write each sentence on your paper. Circle the adjectives. Draw a line under each noun.

1) Long, yellow pencils break.

2) Fat, red apples fall.

3) Strong, young women win.

4) Round, juicy oranges ripen.

5) Gray sparrows fly.

6) Weary men sleep.

Article
A word that points out a noun.

A, *an*, and *the* are called **articles**. Articles are adjectives. Articles point out nouns. *An* is used before words beginning with *a, e, i, o, u,* and sometimes *h*. *A* is used before words beginning with the other letters. *The* is used before any letter.

EXAMPLES   **An** owl hoots.
A fish jumps.
The horn blows.

Activity C Write the article that belongs with each sentence on your paper.

1) (A, An) deer runs.

2) (An, A) old man sleeps.

3) (An, The) best team wins.

4) (The, A) egg hatches.

5) (The, An) summer breeze blows.

Activity D Add an adjective to each sentence. You may choose from the list below or think of your own. Write the complete sentences on your paper.

a	good	loud	the
an	great	old	tired
big	healthy	pretty	wild
brave	little	strong	young

1) _____ sirens squeal.

2) _____ people walk.

3) _____ bugs crawl.

4) _____ flowers bloom.

5) _____ artists draw.

6) _____ soldiers fight.

7) _____ horses run.

8) _____ farmers plant.

Verb

A word that shows action.

Action verb

A word that tells what the subject of a sentence does.

A **verb** is a word that shows action. Verbs tell what is happening in a sentence. The predicate of a sentence always has a verb.

Action verbs tell what the subject does.

EXAMPLE

Ice cream melts.

Part of speech:	*adj.*	*noun*	*verb*

Part of speech: *adj. noun verb*

Parts of sentence: subject | predicate

Sentence pattern: subject + verb

(*Melts* tells what the cream does. *Melts* is an action verb.)

Activity A Write each sentence on your paper. Draw a line under each action verb.

1) The red rooster crows.

2) The golden sun rises.

3) An old, rusty bell clangs.

4) A lonely bird sings.

5) A new day dawns.

Action verbs do not always show action or movement.

EXAMPLE

The tired dog sleeps.

(*Sleeps* is an action verb. There's not any real action in *sleeps*, but it still tells what the dog—the subject—does.)

Activity B Write each sentence on your paper. Draw a line under each action verb.

1) The gray kitten breathes.

2) The drowsy owls stare.

3) A wise old man sits.

4) An athlete rests.

5) Little children dream.

Activity C Complete each sentence with an action verb that makes sense. Choose one of the verbs in the box below or think of your own. Write the complete sentences on your paper.

cries	strikes	sets	laughs
rises	hops	reads	jokes
grows	races	studies	plays

1) The white rabbit _____ .
2) The red sun _____ .
3) A tiny leaf _____ .
4) A happy clown _____ .
5) A lost child _____ .
6) The small plant _____ .
7) The student _____ .
8) Bright lightning _____ .

Activity D Write each sentence on your paper. Label each word a noun (*n.*), an adjective (*adj.*), or a verb (*v.*).

Example   An eel slithers.
            adj. n. **v.**

1) The young racehorse trots.
2) A fat robin chirps.
3) An owl sleeps.
4) A friend waves.
5) A black kitten drinks.

Activity E Write the answer to each question.

1) What does an action verb tell?
2) What does a noun tell?
3) What does an adjective tell?

Adverb

A word that describes
a verb, an adjective,
or another adverb.

An **adverb** is a word that describes a verb, an adjective, or another adverb. When an adverb describes a verb, it tells how, when, or where. In this lesson, adverbs tell *how* about verbs.

EXAMPLE

Ice cream melts quickly.

Part of speech:	*adjective*	*noun*	*verb*	*adverb*

Parts of sentence: subject | predicate

Sentence pattern: subject + verb

(The adverb *quickly* tells **how** the ice cream melts.
Quickly is an adverb used to describe the verb *melts*.
Quickly is part of the predicate.)

Activity A Write each sentence on your paper. Circle each adverb. Draw a line under the verb it tells about.

1) The brown deer ran swiftly.

2) The train whistle blows loudly.

3) The snow falls quickly.

4) The bus moves rapidly.

5) The couple dances gracefully.

All of the adverbs in Activity A come after the verb. Adverbs do not always come after a verb. Wherever an adverb that describes the verb comes in a sentence, it is part of the predicate.

EXAMPLE

adj.   *adj.*   *noun*   *verb*   *adverb*
The brown deer | ran swiftly.

Parts of sentence: subject | predicate

subject
Swiftly, | the brown deer | ran.
predicate

(The adverb *swiftly* tells **how** about the verb *ran* in both sentences. *Swiftly* is separated from the verb *ran* in the second sentence, but it is still part of the predicate.)

Activity B Write the Activity A sentences again. This time, begin each sentence with the adverb.

All of the adverbs in Activity A end in *-ly*. Some examples of adverbs that do not end in *-ly* are *fast*, *hard*, and *well*. These adverbs usually come after the verb.

Activity C Write each sentence on your paper. Draw a line under the verb. Circle the adverb.

1) The whole team plays hard.

2) The track star runs fast.

3) A bird sings well.

4) The teacher spoke fast.

5) The young people work hard.

6) The man dresses well.

7) The couple dances well.

8) The waiter serves fast.

People sometimes mix up the words *good* and *well*. *Good* is always an adjective. *Well* is usually an adverb.

Activity D In these sentences, *well* is an adverb. *Good* is an adjective. Write these sentences on your paper. Label each word a noun (*n.*), a verb (*v.*), an adjective (*adj.*), or an adverb (*adv.*).

Example   The good athlete runs well.
              adj. adj.   n.   v.   adv.

1) A good idea does well.

2) Good steak cooks well.

3) A good old recipe works well.

4) A good student learns well.

5) A good car drives well.

Adverbs tell how, when, or where an action happens. In this lesson, adverbs tell *when* about verbs.

> **EXAMPLE**   Ice cream melts now.
> | | | |
> Parts of speech: *adjective noun verb adverb*
>
> Parts of sentence: subject | predicate
>
> Sentence pattern: subject + verb
>
> (*Now* is an adverb used to describe the verb *melts*.
> *Now* tells **when** the ice cream *melts*.)

Activity A Write each sentence on your paper. Circle each adverb. Draw a line under each verb.

  1) The jet plane lands today.

  2) The wide river floods often.

  3) The guest arrives tomorrow.

  4) The old bus stops twice.

  5) The TV shows run again.

  6) A good worker tries again.

  7) The mail comes early.

  8) The morning paper comes late.

  9) A good friend arrives today.

 10) The clock stops sometimes.

 11) The store closes soon.

 12) The sick child coughs often.

 13) A little girl laughs first.

 14) A kind nurse visits daily.

 15) The angry dog barks now.

As you learned in Lesson 5, adverbs do not always come after the verb. Some sentences begin with adverbs.

> **EXAMPLE** **Today,** the space shuttle lands.
>
> (*Today* is an adverb telling when the space shuttle lands.)

Activity B Write the Activity A sentences again. Begin each sentence with the adverb. Write the new sentences on your paper.

Sometimes adverbs come right before the verb.

> **EXAMPLE** The friends **often** travel.
>
> (*Often* is an adverb telling when the friends travel.)

A sentence can have more than one adverb. Adverbs can begin or end a sentence. An adverb can come before or after the verb.

> **EXAMPLES** The bus **always** arrives **late.** People wait **sometimes.** **Often** people leave.

Activity C Write each sentence on your paper. Circle each adverb. Draw a line under each verb. Some sentences may have more than one adverb.

1) The baseball game starts late.

2) The pitcher suddenly throws.

3) The batter swings once.

4) A player runs fast.

5) Soon the best team wins.

6) The team sometimes practices early.

Adverbs tell how, when, or where an action happens. In this lesson, adverbs tell *where* about verbs.

EXAMPLE

Ice cream melts there.

Parts of speech: *adjective noun verb adverb*

Parts of sentence: subject | predicate

Sentence pattern: subject + verb

(*There* tells **where** the ice cream melts. *There* is an adverb that describes the verb *melts.*)

Activity A Write each sentence on your paper. Circle the adverb. Draw a line under the verb.

1) Life goes on.
2) A football player falls down.
3) The fire truck drives nearby.
4) The computer sits downstairs.
5) An airplane takes off.
6) A young couple goes out.
7) A sick man rests upstairs.
8) A new topic came up.
9) A big dog barks outside.
10) The days speed by.
11) The cat stays inside.
12) The tall woman points there.
13) A small plane flew around.
14) The group follows along.
15) The sleepy captain goes below.

Activity B Read each sentence and find each adverb. Write each adverb on your paper. Write whether the adverb tells *how, when,* or *where.* Some sentences may have more than one adverb.

1) Suddenly, news arrives.
2) People often talk.
3) News travels fast.
4) Ships rarely sink.
5) Planes arrive early.
6) Space shuttles speed skyward.
7) Good news reads well.
8) Trains run slowly.
9) Now cars speed nearby.
10) Speed records move up quickly.
11) Sometimes, the computer screen goes blank.
12) A gray squirrel climbs up.

Activity C Number your paper from 1 to 12. Read each sentence and find all the adverbs. Write the adverbs on your paper.

1) Tonight, the late TV show comes on.
2) The old movie stars act well.
3) The pilot flies alone.
4) His instruments work poorly.
5) His fuel runs low.
6) Suddenly, a rescue ship comes.
7) The pilot leaves safely.
8) He smiles happily.
9) Then the TV show ends quickly.
10) The silly ad runs twice.
11) Frequently, the old car stalls.
12) Tomorrow, the bus comes early.

Complete predicate
The whole part of a sentence that tells what the subject is doing.

Complete subject
The whole part of a sentence that tells who or what the sentence is about.

Simple predicate
One or more verbs in a sentence.

Simple subject
One or more subject nouns or pronouns in a sentence.

You have learned that every sentence has a subject and a predicate. The **complete subject** is the whole part of the sentence that tells who or what the sentence is about. The **simple subject** is the one or more main nouns or pronouns in the sentence.

The **complete predicate** is the whole part of the sentence that tells what the subject is doing. The **simple predicate** is the one or more main verbs in the predicate.

EXAMPLE   Cold, hard ice melts slowly.

Parts of sentence: subject | predicate

(*Ice* is the simple subject. *Cold, hard ice* is the complete subject. *Melts* is the simple predicate. *Melts slowly* is the complete predicate.)

Sometimes the simple subject is also the complete subject. Sometimes the simple predicate is also the complete predicate.

EXAMPLE   Ice melts.

Parts of sentence: subject | predicate

(*Ice* is the simple subject and also the complete subject. *Melts* is the simple predicate and also the complete predicate.)

Activity A Write each sentence on your paper. Draw a line under the complete subject. Circle the complete predicate.

1) The rusty car clatters loudly.

2) A skilled worker finishes quickly.

3) The old bicycle breaks suddenly.

4) The tired men work hard.

5) The summer sun shines brightly.

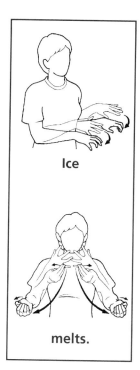

Ice

melts.

Ice melts.

Activity B The complete subject is underlined in each of the following sentences. Number your paper from 1 to 5. Write the simple subject in each complete subject.

1) <u>The black smoke</u> drifts up.

2) <u>A red car</u> stops suddenly.

3) <u>The new clothes</u> fit nicely.

4) <u>A hungry cat</u> eats quickly.

5) <u>A graceful white swan</u> swims fast.

Activity C The complete predicate is underlined in each of the following sentences. Number your paper from 1 to 5. Write the simple predicate in each complete predicate.

1) The kind teacher <u>grades easily</u>.

2) The sharp pencil <u>writes well</u>.

3) The old jeans <u>fade nicely</u>.

4) The large theater <u>quickly fills</u>.

5) The orange leaves <u>fall slowly</u>.

Activity D Copy these sentences on your paper. Underline the complete subject once and the complete predicate twice. Circle the simple subject and simple predicate.

1) The large mall fills quickly.

2) A bright, young couple shops carefully.

3) The small child cries loudly.

4) Shiny, new products sell easily.

5) A polite guard helps quietly.

Not all groups of words tell a complete idea. Groups of words that do not tell a complete idea are called **fragments**. A fragment is missing a subject or a predicate. Because a fragment does not tell a complete idea, it is not a sentence.

Fragment

A group of words that is not a complete sentence.

EXAMPLES   Fragment: Cold, hard ice.

(What happened to *Cold, hard ice*? This fragment is missing a predicate.)

Fragment: Melts slowly.

(What *Melts slowly*? This fragment is missing a subject.)

Sentence: Cold, hard ice melts slowly.

Activity A On your paper, write the groups of words that are complete sentences. Begin each sentence with a capital letter. End each sentence with a period.

1) kites fly
2) the young people
3) small, distant kites
4) other people watch
5) long kite string
6) flying high
7) the boys play
8) clear, sunny day
9) it goes far
10) fun there
11) race cars
12) cars race
13) the finish line
14) friends cheer
15) the day ends

Activity B Decide whether each group of words is missing a subject or a predicate. Complete each fragment and write it as a sentence on your paper.

1) a tall, thin boy

2) drove yesterday

3) dropped quickly

4) the happy woman

5) big, white waves

6) jumped up quickly

7) the wet, foggy, cold night

8) the beautiful flower garden

9) played softly

10) slept peacefully

Activity C Read the short passage. Then follow the directions.

> A big, red kite. An old green kite rises slowly.
> Suddenly, the long string breaks. Disappears quickly.

1) Find two fragments in the passage. Copy them on your paper. Beside each fragment, write whether it is missing a subject or a predicate.

2) Complete each fragment to make it a sentence. Add a subject or predicate. Write the new sentences on your paper.

3) Find two complete sentences in the passage. Copy them on your paper. Underline the complete subject once and the complete predicate twice in each sentence. Circle the simple subjects and simple predicates.

Punctuation

Marks in a sentence that tell readers when to pause or stop.

Comma (,)

A punctuation mark used to set apart one or more words.

You have learned that each sentence begins with a capital letter and ends with a period, question mark, or exclamation point. These marks are kinds of **punctuation**. Punctuation marks are marks that tell readers when to pause or stop.

Commas are another kind of punctuation. They are used in a sentence to set apart one or more words. A comma tells you to pause a brief moment.

A comma can be used to separate two or more adjectives in a sentence.

> **EXAMPLE**   The old, blue car crashed.
>
> (The comma separates *old* and *blue*. *Old* and *blue* are two adjectives that tell about the noun *car*.)

Activity A Write each sentence on your paper. Add commas to separate adjectives.

1) A beautiful sunny day dawned.

2) The young lean athlete ran.

3) The excited friendly crowd cheered.

4) A confident happy coach watched.

5) A tired victorious girl rested.

6) The bright shiny medal sparkled.

A comma can be used after an adverb at the beginning of a sentence.

> **EXAMPLES**   Cheerfully, the boy sang.
>
> (The comma separates the adverb *cheerfully* from the rest of the sentence.)

Activity B Write each sentence on your paper. Add commas after adverbs at the beginning of sentences.

1) Sadly the lost boy cries.

2) Immediately a police officer arrives.

3) Soon a crowd gathers around.

4) Nervously the parents search.

5) Loudly they call out.

6) Happily the family hugs.

Activity C Write each sentence on your paper. Add commas where necessary.

1) The long windy road curves sharply.

2) Usually people drive slowly.

3) A young inexperienced driver crashes.

4) Luckily the driver walks away.

5) The older understanding officer helps out.

6) Softly the driver apologizes.

Activity D Write the following sentences on your paper. Begin each sentence with a capital letter. End each sentence with a period. Add commas where necessary.

1) dark heavy clouds gather

2) loud noisy thunder crashes

3) soon lightning strikes

4) the frightened worried people rush inside

5) suddenly rain falls

6) the fierce dangerous storm passes quickly

Part A Answer each question on your paper.

1) Which are the two parts of every sentence?
2) Which part of speech tells the action?
3) Which part of speech tells how, when, or where?
4) Which part of speech names a person, place, or thing?
5) Which part of speech describes nouns?

Part B Read each sentence. Write each simple subject and simple predicate on your paper.

6) The young boy shouts loudly.
7) The wild wolves suddenly howl.
8) The cold, hard wind blows.
9) Slowly, snow falls.
10) The quiet forest grows dark.

Part C Write each sentence on your paper. Underline the complete subject. Circle the complete predicate.

11) The bright, blue truck slows down.
12) A young doctor studies quietly.
13) The new car stops suddenly.
14) The sleepy dog lies down.
15) The new seeds grow fast.

Part D List the nouns and adjectives in these sentences on your paper. Some sentences may have more than one adjective.

16) The radio station plays softly.
17) Rock music videos entertain greatly.
18) The old, worn-out stereo speakers crackle loudly.
19) New electric guitars play well.
20) Finally, the tape stops.

Part E Read each group of words. Decide if each is a sentence or a fragment. Write *sentence* or *fragment* on your paper.

21) New music videos.

22) A new lamp.

23) Rusty hinges creak.

24) Computer software helps.

25) Bright, shiny, yellow bike.

26) An owl hoots.

27) Green grass grows.

28) Moves slowly up above.

29) A brand-new CD player.

30) The bank door.

Part F Write each sentence correctly on your paper. The sentences need capital letters and periods. Some sentences need commas.

31) the skillful builder works hard

32) the tired worker tries again

33) suddenly the new saw breaks

34) carefully the worker saws again

35) the old wood splits

Test Taking Tip Do you have vocabulary to learn? Make flash cards. Write a word on the front of each card. Write the definition on the back. Use the flash cards to test your skills.

Chapter

2

Adding Prepositions

Have you ever lost a set of keys? You look all over for them. You go back to all the places you have been. You picture in your mind the last time you had the keys. At last you find them! They were under some papers. Or they were behind a book. Or they were inside a pocket. The words *under, behind,* and *inside* tell where the keys were in relation to papers, a book, or a pocket.

In this chapter, you will study words that help show the relationship between things.

Goals for Learning

▶ To identify and use prepositions and prepositional phrases

▶ To state the use of prepositional phrases

▶ To tell the difference between prepositions and adverbs

▶ To identify state-of-being verbs

▶ To use capital letters with proper nouns

▶ To use a comma to set off an introductory prepositional phrase

Preposition

A word that ties or relates a noun or pronoun to another part of the sentence.

Prepositional phrase

A group of words that begins with a proposition and ends with a noun or pronoun.

Object of the preposition

The noun or pronoun that follows the preposition.

A **preposition** is a word that ties or relates a noun or pronoun to another part of the sentence.

A **prepositional phrase** is a group of words that begins with a preposition and ends with a noun or pronoun. The noun or pronoun that follows the preposition is the **object of the preposition.**

EXAMPLE

Tanya looked **at the car**

Parts of speech: *noun   verb   prep.   adj.   noun*

(The preposition *at* begins the prepositional phrase *at the car.* The noun *car* is the object of the preposition *at.*)

Different prepositions show a different relationship between words in a sentence. Notice how the meaning of the sentence changes when the preposition changes.

EXAMPLES

Tanya looked **inside the car.**

Tanya looked **under the car.**

Tanya looked **behind the car.**

Here are some words commonly used as prepositions.

aboard	behind	from	since
about	below	in	through
above	beneath	inside	to
across	beside	into	toward
after	between	near	under
against	beyond	of	until
along	by	off	up
among	down	on	upon
around	during	outside	with
at	except	over	within
before	for	past	without

Activity A Add a different preposition to each of the following sentences. Write each sentence on your paper.

1) Sam walked _____ the woods.

2) They talked _____ the music video.

3) We sat _____ the shady tree.

4) The plane flew _____ the clouds.

5) The principal spoke _____ the new students.

6) Lisa jumped _____ the big puddle.

7) The dog ran _____ the yard.

8) A boy waited _____ the park bench.

9) Pete looked _____ the little house.

10) They watched _____ their friends.

As you have seen, prepositions help you add more information to your sentences. Prepositional phrases make your sentences more interesting and complete.

EXAMPLES   The boys swam.

The boys swam **in the pond.**

(The prepositional phrase *in the pond* adds information to the sentence *The boys swam.*)

Activity B Add a prepositional phrase from the box to each sentence. Write the new sentences on your paper. Use each phrase only once.

near the car	along the shore	in the flower garden
for two hours	around the block	with her best friend

1) We searched.

2) Rain fell.

3) Mom works.

4) They talked.

5) Matt drove.

6) Kim walked.

A prepositional phrase can be an adjective phrase or an adverb phrase.

An **adjective prepositional phrase** acts like an adjective in a sentence. Like an adjective, an adjective prepositional phrase describes a noun. It answers the questions *Which one?* or *What kind?* about a noun.

Adjective prepositional phrase

A prepositional phrase that describes a noun.

EXAMPLES

The ice cream **with nuts** melted.

Parts of speech: *adj. adj.*   *noun*   *prep.* *noun*   *verb*

(The preposition *with* shows the relationship of *nuts* to *ice cream*. *With nuts* is an adjective prepositional phrase that answers the question *What kind of ice cream?* The ice cream with nuts.)

The girl **on** **the** **bus** laughed.

Parts of speech: *adj. noun prep. adj. noun verb*

(The preposition *on* shows the relationship of *bus* to *girl*. *On the bus* is an adjective prepositional phrase that answers the question *Which girl?* The girl on the bus.)

You have learned that the complete subject is the whole part of the sentence that tells who or what the sentence is about. The simple subject is the one or more main nouns or pronouns in the subject.

An adjective prepositional phrase that tells about the simple subject is part of the complete subject.

EXAMPLE

Sentence parts: *complete subject*   *predicate*

The girl on the bus laughed.

simple subj.   *adj. prep. phrase*

(The adjective prepositional phrase *on the bus* describes the simple subject *girl*, a noun.)

Activity A Each of these sentences has an adjective prepositional phrase that describes the simple subject. Write each sentence. Underline the adjective phrase. Circle the noun it describes.

Example A young (man) <u>with a camera</u> spoke softly.

1) A dog inside the house barked.

2) A scared woman with a child hurried outside.

3) The firefighters from town arrived quickly.

4) The black smoke from the fire drifted away.

5) A big player with the ball ran quickly.

6) People in the stands cheered loudly.

A prepositional phrase includes the preposition, the object of the preposition, and all of the words in between. Adjectives that come between a preposition and its object tell about the object.

EXAMPLE An old owl in the tall oak tree blinked.

Prep. phrase: in the tall oak tree

Parts of speech: prep. adj. adj. adj. noun

(The adjectives *the, tall,* and *oak* all tell about the noun *tree,* the object of the preposition *in.* The adjectives *an* and *old* tell about the noun *owl,* the simple subject of the sentence.)

Activity B Write each sentence. Underline the adjective prepositional phrase. Circle the noun it describes. Draw an arrow from each adjective to the noun it describes.

Example Small (waves) <u>on the large lake</u> rippled.

1) The strong men in the canoe paddled quickly.

2) Smoke from the big, bright fires drifted upward.

3) The huge pile of wood disappeared.

4) Small boys with happy faces ran swiftly.

5) Three small children on the blanket watched quietly.

Prepositional phrases often come between the simple subject and the verb in a sentence. Don't let the noun or pronoun that is the object of the preposition confuse you. The object of a preposition is *never* the subject of a sentence.

To find the simple subject of a sentence, follow these steps.

1. Find the verb.

2. Ask *who* or *what* is doing the action.

3. Find the noun or pronoun that answers the *who* or *what* question about the verb.

4. Do not include nouns or pronouns that are part of a prepositional phrase.

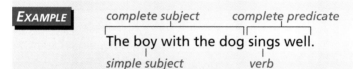

EXAMPLE

complete subject   complete predicate

The boy with the dog sings well.

simple subject   verb

(The words *boy* and *dog* are nouns in the complete subject. To find out which noun is the simple subject ask the question *Who sings well?* The boy does. *Boy* is the simple subject. *Dog* is the object of the preposition *with.* The adjective prepositional phrase *with the dog* describes *boy.*)

Activity A Write each sentence on your paper. Circle the prepositional phrase. Underline the simple subject.

1) The plant with yellow leaves died.

2) The yellow leaves of the dead plant fell softly.

3) The plant near the window grew well.

4) Light from the big window shined brightly.

5) Flowers on the plant opened wide.

6) New leaves on the stems grew steadily.

Some nouns name groups of people or things.

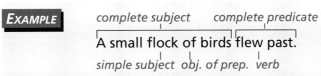

| **EXAMPLES** | group | team | flock | herd |
| | crowd | bunch | collection | class |

When an adjective prepositional phrase follows a word that names a group, you may become confused about which noun is the subject. Remember, the object of a preposition is *never* the subject of a sentence.

EXAMPLE

complete subject   complete predicate

A small flock of birds flew past.

simple subject obj. of prep. verb

(Although *birds* answers the question *What flew past?*, *birds* cannot be the subject because it is the object of the preposition *of*. The noun *flock* is the simple subject. The adjective prepositional phrase *of birds* describes *flock*.)

Activity B Write each sentence. Circle the prepositional phrase. Underline the simple subject.

1) The quartet of men sang loudly.

2) The silent herd of cows moved slowly.

3) A school of green fish flashed past.

4) The collection of precious jewels sparkled.

5) Packs of wild dogs howled.

6) A carton of eggs fell.

Activity C Write each sentence. Fill in the blank with a prepositional phrase to fit the sentence. Draw a line under the simple subject.

1) A team _____ arrived.

2) The happy crowd _____ yelled wildly.

3) A swarm _____ buzzed.

4) A big flock _____ flew away.

5) The new class _____ clapped happily.

6) The fans _____ cheered loudly.

Adverb prepositional phrase

A prepositional phrase that describes a verb.

An **adverb prepositional phrase** acts like an adverb in a sentence. Like an adverb, an adverb prepositional phrase answers the questions *How? When?* and *Where?* about a verb.

EXAMPLES

Ice cream melts quickly **in the sun.**

Parts of speech: adj.   noun   verb   adv.   prep. adj. noun

(The preposition *in* shows the relationship of *sun* to *melts. In the sun* is an adverb prepositional phrase that answers the question *Where does ice cream melt?* In the sun.)

The two girls left **during the game.**

Parts of speech: adj.   adj.   noun   verb   prep.   adj.   noun

(The preposition *during* shows the relationship of *game* to *left. During the game* is an adverb prepositional phrase that answers the question *When did the girls leave?* During the game.)

You have learned that the complete predicate is the whole part of the sentence that tells what the subject is doing. The simple predicate, or verb, is the main verb in the predicate.

An adverb prepositional phrase that tells about the verb is part of the complete predicate.

EXAMPLE

Sentence parts: subject   complete predicate

Ice cream melts quickly in the sun.

verb   adv.   adv. prep. phrase

(The adverb prepositional phrase *in the sun* describes the simple predicate *melts.*)

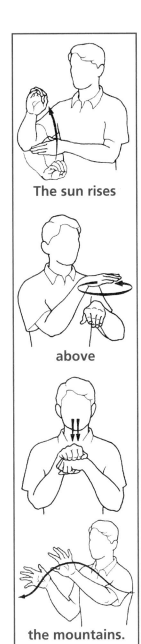

The sun rises

above

the mountains.

The sun rises above the mountains.

Activity A Each of these sentences has an adverb prepositional phrase. Write each sentence. Underline the adverb phrase. Circle the verb it describes. Next to each sentence, write whether the adverb phrase answers *When?* or *Where?* about the verb.

Example   The cowhands (camped) near the stream. *Where?*

1) The campfire burns brightly during the meal.

2) The tired cowhands talk for a little while.

3) Night creeps over the land.

4) Stars shine across the sky.

5) Hot coffee bubbles in the pot.

6) Wolves howl through the still night.

7) Embers glow until morning.

8) The sun rises above the mountains.

9) Another day begins on the range.

Activity B Write each sentence. Fill in the blank with an adverb prepositional phrase that answers the question in parentheses about the verb. Underline the verb.

1) Rick drove directly _____. (Where?)

2) My mom works _____. (When?)

3) The talented musician played _____. (How?)

4) That woman shops daily _____. (Where?)

5) The newborn kitten crawled _____. (Where?)

6) Tina spoke _____. (How?)

Some words that are prepositions can also be adverbs. Remember, a preposition always has an object. An adverb does not have an object.

EXAMPLE

Adverb: The ice cream melted **down**.

Adverb phrase: The ice cream melted **down my arm**.

(In the first sentence, *down* does not have an object. It is an adverb that describes how the ice cream melted. In the second sentence, *down* has an object—*arm. Down* is a preposition that introduces the adverb prepositional phrase *down my arm*.)

Activity A Write the words in bold on your paper. Write whether it is an *adverb* or a *preposition*.

1) The cat looked **around.**

2) The bus traveled **around** the block.

3) The girls waited **outside**.

4) The car parked **outside** the gate.

5) The ball rolled **down** the stairs.

6) Heavy rain poured **down.**

Activity B Write the sentences. Draw one line under the adverb. Draw two lines under the prepositional phrase. Circle the verb.

Example   The rear tire (blows)out on the hill.

1) The driver of the car slows down in seconds.

2) The car stops across from our house.

3) The car sits up on a jack.

4) A bus rattles by past the car.

5) A tow truck comes along after a few minutes.

Activity C Complete each of the sentences below with a word from the box. First use the word as an adverb. Then use the word as a preposition that introduces an adverb prepositional phrase. Do not use a word more than once.

after	around	before	behind	down
inside	near	out	outside	up

Examples   We drove _____ .
                   We drove **around.**
                   We drove **around the block.**

1) The curious boy looked _____.

2) The happy children walked _____.

3) A small, green frog jumped _____.

4) The painter climbed _____.

5) The clumsy clown fell _____.

Activity D Write each sentence on your paper. Circle the prepositional phrase. Above the phrase, write whether it is an adjective phrase or an adverb phrase. Draw an arrow to the subject or the verb that the phrase tells about.

Examples

                             Adv. prep. phrase
A rooster crowed loudly (at dawn.)

              Adj. prep. phrase
A bag (of peanuts) spilled outside.

1) The kind doctor from the village smiled.

2) The big man laughed loudly at the joke.

3) The strong swimmer dove beneath the waves.

4) Ten boxes of books arrived.

5) A small, green bird whistled shrilly for its mate.

6) Thunder boomed across the river.

7) The tree behind our house fell over.

Sentences often have more than one prepositional phrase. Sometimes the phrases describe the same word.

A sentence may have more than one adjective phrase.

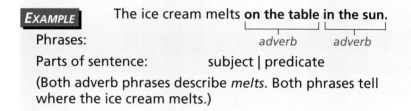

EXAMPLE   The boy **in the first row beside my brother** waved.

Phrases: *adjective*   *adjective*

Parts of sentence: subject | predicate

(Both adjective phrases describe *boy.* Both phrases tell which boy waved.)

A sentence may have more than one adverb phrase.

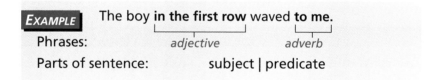

EXAMPLE   The ice cream melts **on the table in the sun.**

Phrases: *adverb*   *adverb*

Parts of sentence: subject | predicate

(Both adverb phrases describe *melts.* Both phrases tell where the ice cream melts.)

A sentence may have adjective phrases and adverb phrases.

EXAMPLE   The boy **in the first row** waved **to me.**

Phrases: *adjective*   *adverb*

Parts of sentence: subject | predicate

You have learned about adjective prepositional phrases that describe subjects. An adjective prepositional phrase may also describe the noun object of another prepositional phrase.

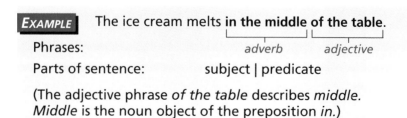

EXAMPLE   The ice cream melts **in the middle of the table.**

Phrases: *adverb*   *adjective*

Parts of sentence: subject | predicate

(The adjective phrase *of the table* describes *middle.* *Middle* is the noun object of the preposition *in.*)

Activity A On your paper, write each prepositional phrase. Then write the word each phrase describes.

1) Ducks swam in the middle of the pond.

2) Flowers sit in the middle of the table.

3) People sit in the middle of the room.

4) A lazy cat sleeps in the middle of the big bed.

5) The old television broke in the middle of a good show.

6) The car with the number on the side stopped.

7) The blind man walked down the street into the park.

8) The people wait in the hall outside the door.

9) The fisher waited along a riverbank at dawn.

10) The new computer waits in the lab for the new student.

Activity B Write the prepositional phrases in each sentence. Next to each phrase write *adjective phrase* or *adverb phrase* and the word the phrase describes.

Example   Workers with briefcases hurry to their office in town.
**with briefcases—adjective phrase, workers
to their office—adverb phrase, hurry
in town—adjective phrase, office**

1) A clerk works quietly at the computer with a smile on his face.

2) Another clerk sorts through a stack of paper carefully.

3) A huge amount of work piles up on the desks for other people.

4) A long line of people waits nervously for reports on the new project.

5) The computer clerks in the office work hard through the long hours of the day.

6) Paper slides off the pile to the floor.

7) Later, the clerks ask for extra pay for the extra hours of work.

State-of-being verb

A verb that tells that the subject exists, but does not show action.

You have learned that an action verb is a word that shows action. There is another kind of verb. It is a **state-of-being verb.** A state-of-being verb tells that the subject exists in some way. A state-of-being verb does not show any action.

Here are some commonly used state-of-being verbs.

am	is	were
are	was	will be

Because a state-of-being verb does not show any action, you may have difficulty finding the verb when it is followed by an adverb prepositional phrase. Remember:

- A verb is never part of a prepositional phrase.
- A prepositional phrase always begins with a preposition.

EXAMPLE The ice cream **is on the table.**

Parts of sentence: *subject verb adverb phrase*

Sentence pattern: subject + verb

(*Is* is a verb. The verb *is* doesn't show action. It tells that the ice cream exists. It is a *state-of-being verb.* The preposition *on* begins the prepositional phrase *on the table.*)

Activity A Write each sentence on your paper. Underline the state-of-being verb. Circle the prepositional phrase.

1) Jack is behind the eight ball.

2) I am in big trouble.

3) The trouble was around the corner.

4) We are in hot water.

5) His problem is at work.

Activity B Write each sentence. Circle the prepositional phrases. Draw one line under the subject noun. Draw two lines under the state-of-being verb.

Example   A bag of <u>nuts</u> <u><u>was</u></u> (in the cupboard.)

1) A pan of brownies is in the oven.

2) The brownies will be on a plate soon.

3) My friends were in the other room.

4) The smell of the warm brownies is in the air.

5) Now my friends are in the kitchen.

6) Sheila was upstairs in her room.

7) My parents were in the basement.

8) The brownies with nuts were on the table.

9) Soon, only crumbs will be in the dish.

Good writers often use action verbs instead of state-of-being verbs. Action verbs make sentences more interesting and more precise than state-of-being verbs do.

EXAMPLES

State-of-being verb: The coach **is** in the dugout.

Action verb: The coach **paces** in the dugout.

(The action verb *paces* gives readers a clearer picture of what the coach is doing in the dugout.)

Activity C Write these sentences on your paper. Circle the state-of-being verb in each sentence. Then write the sentence again, using an action verb in place of the state-of-being verb. Try to use a different action verb in each sentence.

1) The pitcher is on the mound.

2) The catcher is behind the plate.

3) Yesterday, Jane was in center field.

4) I am in the stands.

5) Other players are in their dugouts.

6) In a few minutes, they will be on the field.

Prepositional phrases may come anywhere in a sentence. An adjective phrase usually follows the noun it describes. An adverb phrase may come before or after the verb it tells about.

EXAMPLE	**On the road,** a car **with a trailer** stops **near our house.**
Sentence parts:	*adv. phrase* *subject* *adj.phrase* *verb* *adv. phrase*

Activity A Write each sentence. Circle each prepositional phrase. Draw an arrow from the phrase to the word it describes.

Example   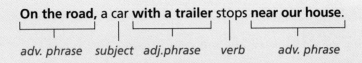 (On the path) a man (with a suitcase) stops.

1) In the front yard of the house, the big dog growls.

2) The mother of the man appears on the porch of the house.

3) The big, old dog lies down in the shade.

4) In the house, the young man visits with his mother.

When you write sentences with prepositional phrases, put each phrase where it makes the most sense.

Activity B Read the facts. Decide which sentence makes more sense. Write the letter of the sentence that makes more sense.

1) Facts The ice cream has nuts. The ice cream melted.

   A) The ice cream with nuts melted.

   B) The ice cream melted with nuts.

2) Facts The man had a dog. The man laughed at a joke.

   A) The man laughed at a joke with the dog.

   B) The man with the dog laughed at a joke.

Activity C Copy the chart shown below on your paper. Then read each sentence and fill in the chart. Like the example, some sentences have more than one prepositional phrase.

Example   A ball player with a good arm pitched well in the ninth inning.

Phrase	Adj. or Adv.	Describes Which Word?	Noun or Verb
with a good arm	adj.	player	noun
in the ninth inning	adv.	pitched	verb

1) Yesterday, a small, yellow airplane landed at the airport.

2) The young tiger leaps through the jungle.

3) The dark blue car with wire wheels parked in the garage.

4) The joggers with red shirts headed through the tunnel.

5) The green boat sliced neatly through the high waves.

6) A short man in a black coat walked toward the light.

7) The boy with a straw hat sits in the sun.

8) The store on the corner opened during the weekend.

9) A duck with a yellow tail swam in the river.

10) A talented little girl sang in a concert at the park.

11) A friend of my mom writes for a newspaper.

12) In the morning, the bus to the airport arrives on time.

13) The list of names slipped under her desk.

<table>
<tr><td>

Common noun

The name of a general type of person, place, or thing.

</td><td>

A **common noun** names a general type of person, place, or thing. A common noun does not begin with a capital letter.

Here are some common nouns.

</td></tr>
</table>

EXAMPLES	state	woman	girl
	man	city	boy

Proper noun

The name of a specific person, place, or thing.

A **proper noun** names a specific person, place, or thing. A proper noun always begins with a capital letter.

EXAMPLES	Texas	Aretha	Linda
	Carlos	Seattle	Jake

Activity A Write this list of words. Use capital letters for proper nouns.

1) bird	**6)** girl	**11)** boy	**16)** tree
2) justin	**7)** brenda	**12)** jackie	**17)** david
3) town	**8)** statue of liberty	**13)** house	**18)** table
4) new york		**14)** miami	**19)** kim
5) city	**9)** tower	**15)** jeff	**20)** zachary
	10) cleveland		

You have learned that a comma sets apart one or more words in a sentence. Use a comma after a prepositional phrase that begins a sentence.

EXAMPLE Under the front steps, the cat lay in the shade.

(A comma follows the prepositional phrase *under the front steps* to set it apart from the rest of the sentence.)

Activity B Write each sentence. Add a comma after the prepositional phrase that begins the sentence.

1) On the branch a bird perched.

2) In the hall friends chatted.

3) At the corner a car stopped.

4) On the television a music video played.

5) In the pond the fish swim.

6) Toward the finish line the athlete ran.

7) Between the blankets the kitten slept.

8) Among the trees the monkeys played.

9) During the spring the weather changes.

10) Above the clouds the plane soared.

Remember these rules when writing sentences.

- Begin every sentence with a capital letter. End every sentence that makes a statement with a period.
- Begin proper nouns with capital letters.
- Do not use capital letters with common nouns.
- Use a comma after a prepositional phrase that begins a sentence.

Activity C Write each sentence correctly with capital letters and commas. Put a period at the end of each sentence.

1) near the phone john waited silently

2) at the park karen skated

3) around the corner david waited with his friends

4) to new york the family traveled often

5) except for dwayne the members of the chorus sang

6) in the harbor the statue of liberty stands

Part A Add a different preposition to each phrase. Write the complete prepositional phrase on your paper.

1) _____ the store

2) _____ the tall building

3) _____ a distant corner

4) _____ the trash can

5) _____ a dark alley

6) _____ the high fence

7) _____ the little house

8) _____ a late dinner

9) _____ the noisy neighbor

10) _____ a broken window

Part B Read this paragraph about a race. Then answer the questions on your paper.

> The sleek cars with skillful drivers race around the track. A green flag waves. The cars roar past. A black car is ahead. The excited crowd jumps up. People cheer for the black car. The driver in the black car wins.

11) Find these words in the story. Tell what part of speech each one is: *sleek, with, black, past, in, up, ahead, cars.*

12) Rewrite the first sentence so that it begins with a prepositional phrase. Remember to use a comma.

13) List all the verbs. There are seven—one in each sentence.

14) Find *for the black car.* What kind of prepositional phrase is it?

15) Find *in the black car.* What kind of prepositional phrase is it?

Part C Write each sentence. Underline each state-of-being verb. Circle each action verb.

16) I go to football games.

17) The games are exciting.

18) Derek sits in the bleachers.

19) We cheer for our team.

20) Our team is good.

21) The halfback is very fast.

22) He runs for a touchdown.

23) The game is over.

24) Our team wins.

25) We are happy.

Part D Write each sentence correctly with capital letters and commas. Don't forget the periods.

26) maria wins

27) after the race people cheer for maria

28) happily joshua smiles at maria with pride

29) the prize trophy waits for maria in the winner's circle

30) for the tv camera maria smiles broadly

31) she talks about the race

32) gladly she looks at joshua

33) maria is in the winner's circle

34) she looks at the trophy

35) tomorrow she races again

Test Taking Tip Study for your test. Review your graded activities and quizzes. The same information may be on the test.

Chapter

3

Using Compound Parts

Have you ever made a list of things to do? Your list might have looked something like this.

> Go to store and buy bread, milk, and yogurt.
> Finish homework and check it.
> Meet Gene and Melanie.

Your list shows that you have more than one thing to do. You have several things to buy. You have homework. You have a couple of people to meet.

In this chapter, you will study sentences with words that connect ideas.

Goals for Learning

▶ To identify and use conjunctions
▶ To identify compound subjects, predicates, and objects of prepositions
▶ To combine two simple sentences using a conjunction
▶ To use commas correctly with compound parts
▶ To capitalize and punctuate titles correctly

> **Conjunction**
>
> A word that joins two or more words, phrases, or ideas in a sentence.

A **conjunction** is a word that joins two or more words, phrases, or ideas in a sentence.

Here are some commonly used conjunctions:

and	but	or
as well as	yet	

EXAMPLES

Words: Pedro **and** Karen went to the mall.
She's my friend **as well as** my sister.

Phrases: Did he go into the house **or** down the street?

Ideas: He travels around the world, **yet** he longs for home.
I tried hard, **but** I lost.

Activity A Write each sentence on your paper. Fill in the blank with a conjunction. Use *and, but, or, as well as,* and *yet.*

1) Tim _____ Lisa will call later.

2) The paper _____ the pencil are on the desk.

3) You should go to bed, _____ you will oversleep.

4) My sister _____ my mother arrived late.

5) The cat moved quickly _____ silently.

6) Cindy _____ Paul cleaned up.

7) His ancestors come from Spain _____ Portugal.

8) They traveled along wide city streets _____ narrow country roads.

9) A girl in running shorts _____ sneakers came to the door.

10) Slowly _____ violently, the storm swept through town.

11) The dog crawled up the stairs _____ into my bed.

Activity B Write each sentence on your paper. Circle the conjunction. Underline the words, phrases, or ideas that the conjunction connects in each sentence.

Examples   Her <u>coat</u> (and) <u>hat</u> are in the closet.

We looked <u>in the box</u> (as well as) <u>on the shelf.</u>

<u>I arrived late,</u> (yet) <u>I sat up front.</u>

1) Old folks as well as teenagers showed up.

2) We spoke to Frank or Anita about the cleaning supplies.

3) Through the day and into the night, we worked.

4) Some people gave up, but we never did.

5) I dusted, and she swept.

6) Slowly but surely the old house came to life.

7) Windows and floors sparkled.

8) The old yet sturdy house stood proudly.

These conjunctions come in sets, but they are separated in a sentence.

both—and	not only—but also
either—or	neither—nor

EXAMPLES	**Both** the ice **and** the ice cream melted.
	Either Jan **or** I will drive.
	Not only Dave **but also** his dad left early.
	Neither my radio **nor** my tape deck worked.

Activity C Write a different set of conjunctions for each sentence.

1) Unfortunately ＿＿ her books ＿＿ her homework were at school.

2) The books were ＿＿ in her locker ＿＿ in the classroom.

3) Ama studied ＿＿ in the evening ＿＿ in the morning before school.

4) Ama ＿＿ rode to school ＿＿ walked.

Compound subject

Two or more subjects joined by a conjunction.

A sentence may have more than one subject. A **compound subject** is two or more subjects joined by a conjunction.

 EXAMPLE   *Frozen sherbet and ice cream* melt in the sun.

compound subject

(This sentence tells about two things that melt in the sun—*sherbet* and *cream*. *Sherbet* and *cream* are a compound subject made up of two simple subjects. They are joined by the conjunction *and*. The complete subject is *Frozen sherbet and ice cream*.)

Activity A Write the complete subject in these sentences on your paper. Underline the simple subjects in the compound subject. Circle the conjunction.

1) An alley and an empty store lie ahead.

2) Old products and dirty supplies sit on the shelves in the store.

3) Workers and helpers clean during the cool morning.

4) The clean, empty street and store fill with shoppers.

5) The busy clerks and pleased shoppers smile at the change in the street.

When writing sentences with compound subjects, make sure the sentences are clear and easy for readers to understand.

EXAMPLE   Red **apples**, purple **plums**, yellow **bananas**, and green **grapes** are on sale.

(*Apples, plums, bananas,* and *grapes* are the simple subjects in the compound subject.)

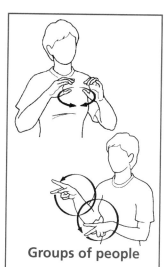

Groups of people

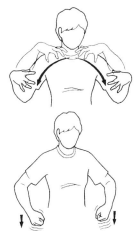

and piles of luggage

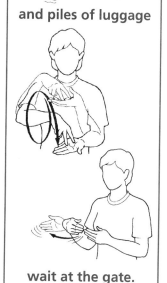

wait at the gate.

Activity B Write the compound subject for each sentence. Underline each simple subject. Circle the conjunction.

1) A duck, a chicken, and a spotted pig stood in the yard.

2) A taxi, a bus, and an old pickup truck drove around the block.

3) A tall lamp, a round table, and a large bed sat in the store window.

4) Kimi, Dawn, and Deepa step into the airplane for a long trip.

5) Groups of people and piles of luggage wait at the gate.

You can often combine the subjects of two or more sentences into a compound subject in one sentence. The new sentence will usually be more interesting to read.

> **EXAMPLES**   Paul talked. Kevin talked.
> **Paul and Kevin talked.**
>
> Cars make smog. Trucks make smog.
> **Cars and trucks make smog.**

Activity C Write each pair of sentences as one sentence with a compound subject.

1) Chris went to the movies. Marco went to the movies.

2) A tape played loudly. A CD played loudly.

3) The old table broke. The old chair broke.

4) The moon shone brightly. The stars shone brightly.

5) Ted works at the bank. Trish works at the bank.

Groups of people and piles of luggage wait at the gate.

A sentence may have more than one predicate.
A **compound predicate** is two or more verbs joined by
a conjunction.

Compound predicate

Two or more predicates joined by a conjunction.

EXAMPLE The ice cream **melted** and **stuck** *to the table.*

compound predicate

(This sentence tells about two things that the ice cream
did—melted and stuck. *Melted* and *stuck* are a
compound predicate made up of two simple predicates,
or verbs. They are joined by the conjunction *and*. The
complete predicate is *melted and stuck to the table*.)

Activity A Write the complete predicate in these sentences
on your paper. Underline the verbs in the compound
predicate. Circle the conjunction.

1) A long train whistles and eases around the curve.

2) Tracks bend and groan under the weight of the train.

3) The slow train rattles and squeaks along the tracks.

4) A startled rabbit jumps up and runs out of the tall
grass.

5) A gentle stream bubbles and splashes over the rocks.

6) Clouds of dust from the train rise and settle on the
road.

7) The long train sways and fades into the distance.

A conjunction may join two, three, four, or more verbs in
the predicate.

EXAMPLE The ice cream **melted, dripped,** and **stuck** *to
the table.*

(*Melted, dripped,* and *stuck* are the verbs in the
compound predicate.)

Activity B Write the complete predicate for each sentence. Underline each simple predicate. Circle the conjunction.

1) Joe sits in the new car, drives along the street, and honks at friends.

2) The young man looks for a store, stops, parks, and walks down the street.

3) Joe goes into the store, looks at the shelves, and talks to the owner.

4) The young buyer laughs, jokes, and pays for a CD.

5) Joe gets into his car, roars past the park, and turns onto the highway.

You can often combine the predicates of two or more sentences into a compound predicate in one sentence. The new sentence will usually be more interesting to read.

 EXAMPLES Brian sat. Brian groaned.
Brian sat and groaned.

Maria cooked dinner. Maria set the table.
Maria cooked dinner and set the table.

Activity C Write each pair of sentences as one sentence with a compound predicate.

1) Mark ate at the counter. Mark drank at the counter.

2) Sue watched television. Sue went to bed.

3) The old dog barked. The old dog howled.

4) The brown rabbit jumped. The brown rabbit ran away.

5) The young women sat at the table. The young women talked at the table.

Some sentences with compound subjects may also have adjective prepositional phrases. The object of a prepositional phrase may be compound, too.

EXAMPLE The **woman** in the coat and hat and the **girl** with the stuffed toy spoke softly.

Compound subject: *woman* and *girl*

Compound object   *coat* and *hat*
of a preposition:

Compound object of preposition

Two or more objects of one preposition joined by a conjunction.

It may seem difficult at first to locate the simple subjects in a sentence with a compound subject, prepositional phrases, and **compound objects of the preposition**. However, there are some steps you can follow to find the subject.

Step 1. Find the verb.

Step 2. Ask who or what is doing the action. (The answer is more than one word if the subject is compound.)

Step 3. Find the prepositions. Remember that the object of a preposition is never the subject.

Activity A Write this sentence. Then follow the directions.

The ice cream with marshmallows and nuts and the frozen yogurt in the pint container melted quickly in the hot sun.

1) Draw a line under the simple predicate.

2) Draw two lines under the complete subject.

3) Write the compound simple subjects. Circle the conjunction.

4) Put brackets [] around the prepositional phrases in the complete subject.

5) Circle the object or compound object of each preposition in the subject.

Activity B On your paper, write the compound simple subjects of each sentence.

1) Diane in a white sweater and Rosa in a blue coat wait outside a theater in the cool breeze.

2) The girls and a few friends talk about the new movie and the actors.

3) Behind the girls, more men, women, and teenagers crowd onto the sidewalk and the street.

4) At the curb, a man in a dark suit and a woman in a pink dress arrive.

5) The girls and the large crowd of men and women cheer for the famous couple.

Activity C Write each verb in the Activity B sentences.

Activity D Write each sentence. Underline the simple subjects.

1) A yellow plane with a number on the wing and a silver plane with a blue design bounce along the rough ground.

2) The model plane with red and green lights glides high above the trees.

3) A wooden plane and a metal plane wait with their owners in the open field of short grass.

4) People with video cameras and newspeople with mikes watch carefully.

5) The silver and blue plane flies high, soars above the trees, and wins easily.

Activity E Write each preposition in the Activity D sentences. After each preposition, write the object of the preposition.

Compound sentence

A sentence made up of two or more complete sentences joined by a conjunction.

A **compound sentence** is made up of two or more sentences joined by a conjunction. A compound sentence joins two related ideas. Each part of a compound sentence has a subject and a verb.

EXAMPLES

Sentence: The ice cream melted.

Sentence parts: *subject*   *verb*

Sentence: The puddle soaked into the cloth.

Sentence parts: *subject*   *verb*

                subject   *verb*

Compound   The ice cream melted, and the
sentence: puddle soaked into the cloth.

            subject   *verb*

(In the compound sentence, the two related ideas are joined by the conjunction *and*. A comma is used before the conjunction to separate the two parts of the compound sentence.)

Activity A   Write the sentences on your paper. Underline the two complete ideas. Circle the conjunction.

Example   A checkered flag falls, (and) the race ends.

1) The winning car rolls across the finish line, and the driver smiles with joy.

2) In the stands, a friend cheers and a brother grins.

3) The driver waves, and the crowd yells louder.

4) On the track, a black car crosses over the line, and a red car limps into the pit.

Activity B Write the subjects and verbs in these sentences on your paper. Write the conjunction that joins the sentence parts.

Example   The wind howls, but the fire burns brightly.

Subjects: **wind, fire**

Verbs: **howls, burns**

Conjunction: **but**

1) The man works on a puzzle, and the woman reads silently in the big chair.

2) The couple sits quietly, and snow piles up on the road.

3) During the storm, the radio crackles, and the lights dim.

4) The long day passes, and darkness falls swiftly.

5) The power fails, but the couple sits warmly by the fire.

6) In the evening, they cook steaks, and the couple eats by candlelight.

7) In the morning, the snow stops, and the power returns.

8) The sun shines brightly, and the snow sparkles.

9) The woman skis on the slopes, yet the man stays in the house.

Activity C Combine each pair of sentences into a compound sentence. Use the conjunction in parentheses. Don't forget to put a comma before the conjunction.

Example   A wolf howled in the darkness.
Michael huddled under the covers. (and)

A wolf howled in the darkness, and Michael huddled under the covers.

1) Shadows moved across the wall.

The door creaked softly. (and)

2) Michael sat up.

The noise faded away. (but)

3) The wind died down.

Michael could not sleep. (yet)

You have learned about compound subjects, compound predicates, compound objects of a preposition, and compound sentences.

Compound

Two or more words, phrases, or ideas joined by a conjunction.

Compounds are two or more words, phrases, or ideas joined by a conjunction. Some sentences have one compound part. Some sentences have two or more compound parts.

Activity A On your paper, write each sentence. Fill in the missing compound shown in parentheses.

1) Nurses watched over the patients during the day and _____. (object of the preposition)

2) The _____ and men walked toward the bus stop. (subject)

3) The bus driver _____ and looked at the train crossing. (verb)

4) Alice and _____ waited for Belinda. (subject)

5) Belinda laughed and _____ to her friends. (verb)

6) The man ate quickly with a knife and _____. (object of the preposition)

7) A car and a _____ turned into the park. (subject)

Activity B Write the compounds found in each of these sentences. Write the kind of compound used.

Example   A team of famous doctors and nurses worked steadily through the night.

       doctors and nurses—objects of the preposition

1) Alberto parked and sat on the pier with his fishing pole.

2) The window fan in the diner blew through the grease and smoke.

3) Crisp, green salads and long pans of tasty meats sat on the table.

4) The fisher with pole, boat, and motor fished in the middle of the river.

Activity C Read each sentence. Write the compound part of each sentence. Then write if it is a *compound subject, compound predicate, compound object of a preposition,* or a *compound sentence.*

1) A gray cat climbed out through a window, and then he ran across the yard.

2) He jumped over the bushes and fence.

3) A small, red car braked and skidded to a sudden stop.

4) The cat jumped through the window of the car, and the driver screamed in fright.

5) The driver and a woman passenger in the car calmly waited for the owner of the cat.

Activity D Read the paragraph. Then write the answer to each item.

> The fish pulled on the hook and line. The fishing rod bent, and the reel buzzed. The fisher and the fish pulled hard. The fisher bent and reached toward the fish. The smart fish scraped against a rock under the water. The fisher stood up, and the fish splashed. Then the rain and wind picked up. Not only the fisher but also the fish headed for home and safety.

1) Write the sentence that has no compounds.

2) What kind of compound does the first sentence have?

3) Write one of the two sentences that has a compound subject but no other compound parts. Underline the simple subjects.

4) Write the sentence that has a compound predicate. Underline the verbs.

5) Write one of the two compound sentences. Underline the two ideas. Circle the conjunction.

6) Find the sentence that has more than one compound part. Write each compound part and its conjunction.

Commas are needed in sentences with three or more compound parts.

> **EXAMPLE**
>
> Dogs often sniff, scratch, bark, or howl.
>
> Parts of speech: *noun   adv.   verb   verb   verb conj. verb*
>
> Parts of sentence: subject | compound predicate

Activity A On your paper, write each sentence. Add commas, capital letters, and periods.

1) carrots corn tomatoes beans and peas grow in the garden

2) spiders flies and mice wait in the basement

3) people eat sleep and rise again for another day

4) swings slides and monkey bars sat on the empty playground

5) cheerleaders bend jump dance and yell

6) toys books and clothes lie on the floor

7) bears snakes and monkeys live in the zoo

8) smoke sparks and flames pour from the chimney

9) trucks buses and cars rumble through the city

Semicolon (;)

A punctuation mark that separates two related ideas not connected by a conjunction.

You have learned that commas are also needed in compound sentences. A comma is placed after the first complete idea, just before the conjunction. A **semicolon** can be used instead of a conjunction to separate two related ideas in a sentence.

> **EXAMPLE**
>
> Some motors hum, but other motors knock.
>
> Some motors hum; other motors knock.

Activity B Write each pair of sentences as one compound sentence. Use a comma with a conjunction in three of the sentences. Use a semicolon in the other two.

1) Skaters glide. Bicyclists ride.

2) The night wind blew. The moon disappeared.

3) Dinner burned in the oven. The smoke alarm rang.

4) The sun shone. People headed toward the beach.

5) Time passed. Night fell.

You know that a proper noun begins with a capital letter. Titles are proper nouns. Titles begin with capital letters.

Titles of books are underlined. In print, they appear in *italic*. The same is true for the titles of magazines, newspapers, and CDs. Each is a complete work. Parts of works such as chapters, articles, and songs need **quotation marks** around them. Remember:

> **Quotation marks**
> (" ")
>
> *Punctuation used around the title of a part of a large work.*

- The title of a large work is underlined or printed in italic.
- The title of a part of a large work is in quotation marks.

> **EXAMPLES** The magazine is <u>Computer World</u>.
>
> The magazine is *Computer World*.
>
> The article is "Using a CD-ROM."

Activity C Correct each sentence. Use capital letters and periods. Underline titles of whole works. Use quotation marks around parts of works.

1) the newspaper is the new york times

2) the book is english to use; the lesson is parts of speech

3) the book is outdoor cookbook; the chapter is cooking chicken

4) the book is fix your car; the chapter is spark plugs

5) the magazine is people; the article is surfing clubs

Part A Read the sentences. Write the conjunctions and the words they connect on your paper.

1) Janet and Maria spent the day at a big park.

2) They looked at animals and shops.

3) They ate hot dogs and popcorn and then went to the rides.

4) The roller coaster was noisy, but it was the most fun.

5) It climbed high and dropped quickly.

6) It whipped around turns and loops.

7) The two friends screamed and yelled.

8) Janet and Maria didn't know what they liked best at the park.

9) Was it the rides or the food?

Part B Write each pair of sentences as a single sentence. Use conjunctions to connect subjects, verbs, or objects of prepositions.

10) Juan goes to the store. Juan goes to the garage.

11) Whitney pulls over in the car. She shouts to her friends on the sidewalk.

12) Irena sings beautifully. Irena dances beautifully.

13) A woman with a large briefcase got on the bus. A boy in a football uniform got on the bus.

Part C Read each sentence. Then answer the questions that follow. Write the letter of the sentences.

> a) An old movie appears on the cable channel.
> b) A man and a woman with a large trunk and a small box wait on a dusty bench inside the station.
> c) The steam engine with the coal car slowly backs onto the main track and connects.
> d) At the station, the man and the woman climb into the train and sit down near a window.
> e) The whistle blows, and the train moves.
> f) TV viewers watch for the hero and the train robbers.

14) Which two sentences have compound verbs?

15) Which sentence has no compounds?

16) Which one is a compound sentence?

17) Which two sentences have compound subjects?

18) Which two sentences have a compound object of a preposition?

19) What part of speech is *man? Small? Into? Down?*

20) Which sentence begins with a preposition?

Part D Write these sentences. Use capital letters and punctuation correctly.

21) the newspaper called usa today lies on the table

22) a paper an old book and a pencil fell on the floor

23) janine jeff and mark talk about sports games and contests

24) the book called computers for everyone has a chapter titled choosing the right machine

25) healthy people eat grains like wheat oats rice and barley

Test Taking Tip Study for your test. Learn the most important facts. Practice writing the material or saying it out loud. Ask a partner to listen. Ask the partner if your answers are right.

Chapter

4

Direct Objects

Have you ever watched an exciting football game? When you are watching a good game, it is sometimes hard to find the player who has the ball. You try to follow the ball from player to player. One player passes the ball. Another player catches the ball. The quarterback hands the ball to someone. Sometimes a player kicks the ball. The ball receives most of the action.

In this chapter, you will study words that take the action of the verb.

Goals for Learning

▶ To identify the *subject + verb + direct object* sentence pattern

▶ To identify simple and compound direct objects

▶ To use pronouns correctly in place of nouns

▶ To capitalize titles of people and abstract proper nouns

▶ To punctuate compound sentences correctly

In earlier lessons, you focused on one sentence pattern: *subject + verb.* Now you will learn about a second sentence pattern: *subject + verb + direct object.*

A **direct object** is a noun or pronoun that receives action directly from the verb.

Direct object

A noun or pronoun that takes action directly from the verb.

EXAMPLES   Sam watched.

Sentence pattern: subject | verb

Sam watched the ball.

Sentence pattern: subject + verb + direct object

(The noun *ball* receives the action of the verb *watched.* Sam watched *what*? Sam watched the ball. *Ball* is the direct object.)

Here are more examples of sentences with action verbs and direct objects. Notice that in each sentence the bold noun takes action directly from the verb.

EXAMPLES

Sentence pattern: subject + verb + direct object.

Lynda set the **table**.

(Lynda set *what*? Lynda set the table. *Table* is the direct object.)

The family ate **dinner**.

(The family ate *what*? The family ate dinner. *Dinner* is the direct object.)

Activity A In each of these sentences, the action verb is in bold. Write the sentences. Draw an arrow from the verb to the direct object.

Example The rain **hits** the ground.

1) A farmer **watches** the rain.

2) The water **washes** the corn.

3) The ground **swallows** the water.

Activity B Fill in the blank with a direct object. Write the completed sentences on your paper.

1) Jim opened the _____ .

2) The baseball hit the _____ .

3) Bright sunlight lit the _____ .

4) A sharp saw cut the _____ .

5) The cat caught a _____ .

Adjectives can describe nouns that are direct objects.

EXAMPLE

Sentence pattern: subject + verb + direct object

The boys watched **an old horror** movie

Parts of speech: *adj.* *noun* *verb* *adj.* *adj.* *adj.* *noun*

(The adjectives *an*, *old*, and *horror* describe the direct object *movie*.)

Activity C Write the sentences. Circle the direct object. Do not include adjectives. Draw an arrow from the verb to the direct object. The verb is in bold.

Example   Thick fog **surrounded** the quiet town.

1) A scientist **pushed** two buttons.

2) Sparks **filled** the cold, dreary room.

3) The scientist **created** a giant monster.

4) The scientist **pushed** another button.

5) The monster **opened** the heavy steel door.

Activity D Write each sentence. Label the subject (*s.*), the verb (*v.*), and the direct object (*d. obj.*)

1) The farmer plowed the muddy field.

2) Ronald hit a long fly ball.

3) Sarah bought an old green book.

4) A brown squirrel climbed a tall oak tree.

5) The shivering boy closed the kitchen window.

Compound direct object

Two or more direct objects joined by a conjunction.

Direct objects can be compound. Two or more direct objects joined by a conjunction make a **compound direct object.**

EXAMPLE   Ice cream stained the cloth and the table.

Parts of speech: *adj. noun   verb adj. noun conj. adj. noun*

Sentence pattern: subject + verb + direct object

(The two nouns *cloth* and *table* receive the action of the verb *stained*. Ice cream stained *what*? Ice cream stained the cloth and table. The nouns *cloth* and *table* make up the compound direct object. They are joined by the conjunction *and*.)

Activity A Write the compound direct object in each sentence. Do not include adjectives.

Example   A storm brings strong winds and heavy rain.
          compound direct object—winds, rain

1) The big storm floods streets and homes.

2) Water fills basements and yards.

3) Big tree limbs block the sidewalks and streets.

4) Cara watches the muddy water and floating branches.

5) A warm sun slowly dries the puddles and mud.

Two sentences with direct objects can be joined to form a compound sentence. Both ideas in the compound sentence will have direct objects.

EXAMPLES   Mai ordered a **sandwich**.
              Tom ordered **soup**.

Compound sentence: Mai ordered a **sandwich**, and Tom
                got **soup**.

(Each part of the compound sentence has a direct object. Mai order *what*? She ordered a sandwich. *Sandwich* is the direct object of the verb *ordered*. Tom got *what*? He got soup. *Soup* is the direct object of the verb *got*. The two ideas are joined by the conjunction *and*.)

Activity B Write these compound sentences. Circle the direct object of each verb. The verbs are in bold.

Example   Steve and Tom **wrote** poor sentences, but they **wanted** good grades.

1) Steve **reads** science fiction stories, but Tom **chooses** war stories.

2) Rosa **played** the piano, and Amy **read** a book.

3) One **likes** music, but the other **likes** books.

4) Rosa **played** loud music, and Amy **covered** her ears.

The direct object follows the verb in a sentence. The direct object is always part of the complete predicate.

EXAMPLE   The people **heard the weather report early.**

Sentence parts: complete subject | complete predicate

Sentence pattern: subject + verb + direct object

(The complete predicate includes the verb *heard* plus the direct object *report* and its adjectives *the weather.* The adverb *early* answers the question *When?* about the verb. *Early* is also part of the complete predicate.)

Activity C Write each sentence. Draw one line under the complete subject. Draw two lines under the complete predicate. Draw a circle around the direct object or compound direct object.

Example   The Weather Channel and the police warned people about a heavy storm.

1) Men, women, and children left the area in their cars.

2) The storm hit the coast and harbors suddenly.

3) The high waves rocked and damaged the boats.

4) Waves and strong winds sank one boat.

5) Thunder and lightning split the sky.

6) A huge wave covered the pier and the beach.

A sentence can have a compound subject, a compound verb, and a compound direct object. Do not confuse sentences with compound parts with compound sentences. Remember, a compound sentence has two complete ideas joined by a conjunction.

EXAMPLES   Ice cream and sherbet stain and soil the cloth and table.

Compound subject: **Ice cream** and **sherbet**

Compound verb: **stain** and **soil**

Compound direct object: **cloth** and **table**

(Although the sentence has compound parts, it does not have two ideas joined by a conjunction. It is not a compound sentence.)

Compound subject: **Ice cream and sherbet stain the cloth,** but **only sherbet stains the cloth and table**.

(This sentence is a compound sentence because it has two ideas joined by the conjunction *but*. The first part of the sentence has a compound subject *ice cream* and *sherbet*. The second part of the sentence has a compound direct object *cloth* and *table*.)

Activity A Number your paper from 1 to 6. Read each sentence. Decide if it is a compound sentence. If it is compound, write *C*. If it is not compound, write *NC*.

1) Cats and dogs scratch and tear rugs and chairs.

2) Maria mowed the lawn, and Joe trimmed the hedge.

3) David and Mark washed and waxed the car and the truck.

4) The driver emptied the trunk, and the friend carried the boxes and bags inside.

5) The farmer and his son fed the pigs and cows, and their guest fed the horses.

6) Lee and Terry cooked and served the dinner.

In sentences that have compound verbs, each verb may have its own direct object.

 EXAMPLE   The cook cleaned the **grill** and flipped **pancakes**.

Compound verb: **cleaned** and **flipped**

(*Grill* is the direct object of *cleaned*. *Pancakes* is the direct object of *flipped*.)

In sentences that have compound verbs, each verb may have a compound direct object.

EXAMPLE   Pat washed the **walls** and **floor** and dusted the **table** and **chairs**.

Compound verb: **washed** and **dusted**

(The compound direct object of *washed* is *walls* and *floor*. The compound direct object of *dusted* is *table* and *chairs*.)

Activity B Number your paper from 1 to 5. Write whether the sentence has a *compound verb, compound direct object,* or *both*.

1) Ben ordered pancakes and eggs.
2) Kim drank coffee and read the morning paper.
3) A server brought the pancakes and poured coffee and juice.
4) Along with his waffle, Eddie wanted strawberries and cream.
5) Ben finished breakfast and left the diner.

Activity C Write if the sentence has a *compound subject, compound verb,* or *compound direct object*. If the sentence is a compound sentence, write *CS*.

1) The birds chirped tunes, and the squirrels gathered nuts.
2) A rabbit ate carrots and lettuce in the garden.
3) The boy and his sister caught fish for dinner.
4) The player removed his hat and glove.
5) Gerri washed the car and tuned the engine.

Direct objects can have prepositional phrases.

> **EXAMPLE**   The sherbet stained the cloth **with fancy lace**.
>
> Sentence pattern: subject + verb + direct object +
>   adjective prepositional phrase
>
> (The adjective prepositional phrase *with fancy lace*
> describes the noun *cloth,* the direct object.)

Activity A Write each sentence. Underline the direct object. Circle the prepositional phrase that tells about the direct object.

Example   Bill read a <u>story</u> (about a fire.)

1) A fire burned a tall building of offices.

2) Workers carried boxes of papers.

3) Firefighters sprayed water from a nearby hydrant.

4) Flames burned the walls inside the building.

5) A brave woman saved a man with a broken leg.

A prepositional phrase that follows a direct object may describe the direct object, or it may describe the verb. Some sentences may have prepositional phrases that describe the direct object *and* prepositional phrases that describe the verb.

> **EXAMPLES**   The hiker carries a pack **with food**.
>
> (The adjective phrase *with food* describes the direct
> object *pack*. It tells which pack. The one with food.)
>
>   The hiker carries a pack **on her back**.
>
> (The adverb phrase *on her back* tells about the verb *carries*.
> It tells where the hiker carries the pack. On her back.)
>
>   The hiker carries a pack **with food on her back**.
>
> (The adjective phrase *with food* describes the direct
> object *pack*. The adverb phrase *on her back* tells about
> the verb *carries*.)

Activity B Write each sentence. Circle each prepositional phrase. Draw an arrow from each phrase to the word it describes.

Example   The rider grabbed the mane (of the horse) (with his right hand.)

1) The horse bucked the rider during the rodeo.

2) The crowd cheered the brave rider on the ground.

3) The horse jumped the fence near the side gate.

4) The rider wiped the dust on his pants with his scarf.

5) Josie met a group of friends after the rodeo.

6) The friends filled a table at the restaurant.

7) A waiter placed glasses of water on the table.

8) Then the waiter took an order for a big batch of ribs.

9) The group of friends tipped the waiter after the meal.

Activity C Make a chart of the prepositional phrases in these sentences. Write the kind of prepositional phrase.

Example   The man with the pole pulled the fish with stripes toward the boat.

Prepositional Phrases	Adjective or Adverb?
with the pole	adjective
with stripes	adjective
toward the boat	adverb

1) The smart fish twisted the line of heavy nylon around a rock.

2) The man in the boat grabbed the line near the surface.

3) The big fish pulled the fisher with all his gear from the small boat.

4) A friend in another boat offered help to the man in the water.

You have learned that nouns can appear in three places in sentences. Nouns can be:

- the subject of a sentence
- the direct object of a sentence
- the object of a preposition

Some sentences have nouns in all three places.

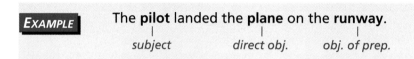

EXAMPLE The **pilot** landed the **plane** on the **runway.**
subject | direct obj. | obj. of prep.

Activity A Write each noun in the following sentences. Next to each noun, write whether it is the *subject, d. obj.,* or *obj. of prep.* (Remember that nouns name persons, places, and things.)

1) The sleek car squealed away from the curb onto the freeway.

2) Craig hit third gear, and the engine howled.

3) A child jumped off the road, away from the car.

4) The gauge on the dash showed an almost empty tank of gas.

5) Craig walked away from the car toward a gas station down the road.

6) People on the ship watched the lights of the city by the harbor.

7) The ship left the harbor and moved toward the sea.

8) Lightning split the sky, and rain drenched the ship.

9) During the storm, a lamp fell from the table in a shower of sparks.

10) The captain steered the ship to another safe harbor.

Concrete noun

A word that names something that can be seen or touched.

Abstract noun

A word that names something that cannot be seen or touched.

Many things that nouns name can be seen and touched, such as *store, book, dog*. Some things cannot be seen or touched, such as *dream, idea, time*. A **concrete noun** names something that can be seen or touched. An **abstract noun** names something that cannot be seen or touched. Here are some examples.

Concrete Nouns	Abstract Nouns
fire	heat
food	hunger
book	idea
baseball	sport
movie	fun

How can you be sure a word is a noun? Remember that articles (*a, an, the*) point out common nouns. If you can use an article with it, the word is a noun.

Activity B Write each noun in these sentences. Tell whether it is concrete or abstract.

1) Chuck had a dream about a horse.
2) The heat from the fire warmed the campers.
3) The bell on the wall made a sound.
4) Anita took time off from work.
5) Tom saw hunger in the eyes of the kitten.
6) Kisha loved the fun and excitement of football.
7) Light from the TV filled the room.
8) Karen had an idea for a game.
9) Bill saw love in the eyes of the old dog.
10) The video filled Joe with fear.

A **pronoun** is a word that replaces a noun in a sentence.

Pronoun

A word that takes the place of a noun.

EXAMPLE   Ice melts quickly in the sun.

It melts quickly in the sun.

Sentence parts: subject | predicate

Sentence pattern: subject + verb

(*Ice* is a noun. *It* is a pronoun. In the second sentence, the pronoun *it* replaces the noun *ice*.)

Pronouns have different forms, or cases.

Pronouns		
	Nominative	**Objective**
One		
First person	I	me
Second person	you	you
Third person	he, she, it	him, her, it
Two or More		
First person	we	us
Second person	you	you
Third person	they	them

Nominative pronoun

A pronoun used as the subject of a sentence.

A **nominative pronoun** replaces a noun used as the subject of a sentence.

EXAMPLE   Rosalie threw a ball to Ricky.

She threw a ball to Ricky.

Objective pronoun

A pronoun used as an object.

An **objective pronoun** replaces a noun used as the direct object or object of the preposition.

EXAMPLES

Rosalie threw a **ball** to Ricky.

Rosalie threw **it** to Ricky.

Rosalie threw a ball to **Ricky**.

Rosalie threw a ball to **him**.

More than one pronoun can be used in a sentence.

EXAMPLE

She threw **it** to **him**.

Activity A For each sentence, choose the correct pronoun. Write the pronoun on your paper and tell what part of the sentence it is.

Example   (We, Us) heard the doorbell ring.
              We—subject

1) (She, Her) looked through the window and saw (they, them) in the rain.

2) Quickly, (I, me) opened the door for (they, them).

3) (He, Him) waited for (we, us) at home.

4) The roof leaked water on (they, them) and dropped plaster on (she, her) and (I, me).

5) (We, Us) left the house, and dark storm clouds dumped rain on (we, us).

6) (We, Us) and (they, them) ran to the bus.

7) The bus dropped some of (they, them) off at the corner.

8) (We, Us) rode with (she, her) to another street.

9) The bus left (he, him) and (we, us) on the curb.

10) Then (he, him) and (I, me) walked through the rain to a shelter with (she, her).

11) After the storm, (we, us) went to my house.

Pronouns help you avoid repeating the same nouns over and over again. They help your sentences sound better.

EXAMPLES
Ed and Al went for a ride Sunday afternoon. Suddenly, **Ed and Al** spotted a turtle in the road. **Ed and Al** stopped and watched the **turtle**.

Ed and Al went for a ride Sunday afternoon. Suddenly, **they** spotted a turtle in the road. **They** stopped and watched **it**.

(In the second group of sentences, the repeated nouns are replaced with pronouns. The pronouns make the sentences sound more like natural speech.)

Do not use pronouns unless readers will know exactly which noun the pronoun is replacing. Sometimes, for clarity, it may be better to repeat the noun.

EXAMPLE
Jon met Paul at the mall. **He** worked there.

(*Who* worked at the mall? Jon or Paul? In this case, the pronoun makes the meaning of the sentence unclear. It would have been better to repeat the noun *Paul*.)

Activity A Write each sentence. Change the words in bold to pronouns. Be sure to use the correct form of the pronoun. Look at the table in Lesson 6 for help.

1) **Josh and Andrea** walked into the busy store and saw Maria and Carlos.

2) Josh met **Maria and Carlos** at the cash register.

3) **Maria** bought a bag of chips.

4) Maria chatted with **Andrea.**

5) Carlos talked to **Josh** about the soccer game.

6) The clerk filled the bag and gave **the bag** to Carlos.

7) **Carlos** walked Josh and Andrea to the car.

8) Josh bought an apple and ate **the apple** on the bus.

Some pronouns end with -self.

myself	himself	themselves
ourself	herself	ourselves
yourself	yourselves	itself

Activity B Write each sentence. Fill in the blank with the correct -self pronoun.

1) I did it by _____ .

2) She did it by _____ .

3) He did it by _____ .

4) You did it by _____ .

5) They did it by _____ .

6) We did it by _____ .

7) It fell all by _____ .

Some pronouns refer to things and people in general. No specific person or thing is pointed out.

People		Things
someone	somebody	something
anyone	anybody	everything
everyone	everybody	anything
no one	nobody	nothing

Activity C Write each pronoun in these sentences. Write whether the pronoun is a *subject, direct object,* or *object of a preposition.*

1) In a small town, everyone knows everything about everybody.

2) In a big city, hardly anyone knows anything about anybody.

3) Someone knows everything about somebody.

4) Everyone knows something about somebody.

Some words in the English language can be used as more than one part of speech.

These words can be used as pronouns or adjectives.

other	another	some
several	many	one (or any other number)
any	few	
each	all	

EXAMPLES   Adjective: **Some** ice melted.

Pronoun: **Some** melted.

(In the first sentence, *some* is an adjective used to describe the noun subject *ice*. In the second sentence, *some* is a pronoun that takes the place of the noun subject *ice*. *Some* is the subject of the sentence.)

Some pronouns are made up of two words.

each other	one another

EXAMPLES   Sheila and Beth call **each other** every day.

Sheila and Beth call **one another**.

Activity A On your paper, write each adjective and the noun it describes.

1) Many people work two jobs.

2) Some men work at several jobs.

3) Each person tries all kinds of jobs.

4) One woman tried ten jobs.

5) Another woman wanted any job.

Activity B Copy each word in bold. Then tell whether it is an *adjective* or a *pronoun.*

1) **Some** people like football games.

2) I like a **few** of them.

3) Sarah likes **some** kinds of sports.

4) We see **several** during each season.

5) She saw **two** in the fall.

6) **Many** people watch football on cable TV.

7) The players tackle **each other.**

8) Good players on a team play well and share the glory with **one another.**

Activity C Use each of these words as a pronoun in a sentence.

1) each other

2) ten

3) anybody

4) several

5) everybody

6) another

7) one another

8) each

9) nothing

10) some

Activity D Use each of these words as an adjective in a sentence.

1) ten   **3)** another   **5)** some

2) several   **4)** each

This, *that*, *these*, and *those* can be used as more than one part of speech. They can be used as either pronouns or adjectives.

EXAMPLES   Adjective: **This** ice cream melted on the table.

Pronoun: **This** melted on the table.

(In the first sentence, *this* is an adjective used to describe the noun subject *ice cream*. In the second sentence, *this* is a pronoun that takes the place of the noun subject *ice cream*. *This* is the subject of the sentence.)

Activity A Write the adjective that describes each noun in bold.

1) This **store** has many items for sale.

2) That **music box** plays a tune.

3) This **chair** has a new cover.

4) This **mirror** shines brightly in that **light.**

5) That **watch** keeps good time.

6) Those **lamps** go nicely with that **table.**

7) These **candles** burn well.

8) This **pen** matches that **pencil.**

Activity B Copy each word in bold. Then write whether it is an *adjective* or *pronoun*.

1) **That** book dropped to the floor.

2) I want **this.**

3) **These** belong on the shelf.

4) Tim will wrap **those** packages for you.

5) Julio lost **that** on the bus.

6) Ali caught **this** fish by herself.

This, that, these, and *those* are used to point out persons and things.

This points out one person or thing that is near. *That* points out one person or thing that is in the distance.

> **EXAMPLES**   **This** girl beside me won the race.
>
> **That** boy by the fountain ran the race.

These points out more than one person or thing that is near. *Those* points out more than one person or thing that is in the distance.

> **EXAMPLES**   **These** people over here served the food.
>
> **Those** people near the door cleaned up.

Activity C Write each sentence. Fill in the blank with *This, That, These,* or *Those.*

Example   Thing: pictures near you

   These   hang on the wall.

1) Thing: vase across the room

   _____ sits on the table.

2) Thing: rug near you

   _____ lies on the floor.

3) Thing: tall plants across the room

   _____ stand in the corner.

4) Thing: curtains near you

   _____ hang at the window.

5) Thing: clock near you

   _____ goes on the shelf.

6) Thing: sofa across the room

   _____ stands along the wall.

Proper nouns can give examples of abstract nouns.
Remember that all proper nouns need capital letters.

Abstract Nouns	Proper Nouns
day	Tuesday
holiday	New Year's Day
event	Super Bowl
language	Spanish

Activity A On your paper, write a proper noun to match
each common noun.

1) day   **5)** event

2) country   **6)** movie

3) holiday   **7)** language

4) water   **8)** baseball team

The name of a person is a proper noun. A person's title is
part of his or her name. **Capitalize** a person's title. To
capitalize, use capital letters. When a short form is used, a
period is needed.

Capitalize

To use capital letters.

EXAMPLES	President Lincoln	Dr. Mary Chang
	Queen Anne	Ms. Ann Kunz
	Prince William	Mrs. Emily Wu
	Senator Jane Brown	Mr. Ed Connors

Activity B Write this list of words. Capitalize each proper
noun. Some of the words are common nouns. Common
nouns do not have capital letters.

1) mr. smith   **6)** movie

2) detroit   **7)** senator

3) statue of liberty **8)** dr. adams

4) school   **9)** day

5) monday   **10)** president washington

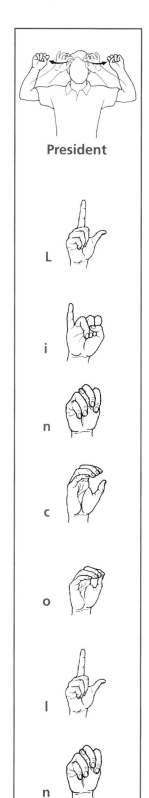

President

L

i

n

c

o

l

n

President Lincoln

Semicolons and commas are needed in compound sentences that use these conjunctions: *however, therefore, besides, instead.*

A semicolon comes before the conjunction. A comma comes after the conjunction.

EXAMPLE The ice cream melted; however, I wiped it up.

Activity C Write each sentence. Add capital letters, commas, semicolons, and periods to make the sentences correct.

1) it rained therefore we left early

2) he wanted candy instead he ate fruit

3) ann brought her car besides we rode with her before

4) the sun set a new moon rose

5) dr adams mr allen and ms romone met senator lopez in the park

6) mr samuels beeped the horn however ms tompkins and mrs west had already left.

7) mrs gomez greeted senator andrews during the labor day parade

8) mr edwards and ms keller watched prince charles on television

9) dr finch opened the door therefore mr lee handed him the package for mrs finch.

10) senator hoober explained the problem to mr boyd ms lake mr shobe and dr connors

Part A Write each sentence. Circle the verb. Draw an arrow to the direct object.

1) The students cleaned the vacant lot.
2) They picked up the trash.
3) The students raked the dirt.
4) Later, they planted some flowers.
5) The students made a new park.

Part B Write each sentence. Replace each noun in bold with a pronoun.

6) **Sara** didn't like **the homework.**
7) Studying for **the test** was hard.
8) **Paul and Nikka** worked together.
9) **Greg** studied with **Franklin and Ramon.**
10) **The students** were all ready for **the test.**

Part C Write a proper noun for each common noun. Be sure to capitalize each proper noun.

11) month
12) state
13) landmark
14) book
15) television show
16) basketball team
17) mountain
18) city
19) car
20) person

Part D Write each sentence. Use capital letters and punctuation correctly.

21) the party honored king armand however king george brought queen anne

22) ms allen met dr gibbs on monday

23) we saw santa claus at the christmas party

24) i have an appointment on tuesday march 17

25) we grabbed our lunches ran out the door and got on the bus

Part E Read this paragraph. Then follow the directions for each item.

> Michelle plays the flute, and Linda plays the guitar. The women often meet and practice music. Linda and Michelle strum and toot songs and tunes. Sometimes a friend stops by, holds the music, and sings a tune with them. Michelle, Linda, and the friend make a good sound and have fun during lazy summer nights.

26) Write the sentence that has a compound subject, compound verb, and compound direct object.

27) Write the compound sentence.

28) Find each of these words and tell its part of speech: *often, Sometimes, practice, with, lazy, and.*

29) Which of these words are abstract nouns? *Michelle, guitar, sound, and, friend, fun.*

30) List the verbs along with any direct objects in the sentence that begins with an adverb.

Test Taking Tip

Do not wait until the night before to prepare for a test. Study for a short time every day. Plan your study time. Get a good night's sleep on the night before a test.

TOSSED FRESH ALL DAY!

Choice of

Practice With Parts of Speech

Do you remember how you learned to do something new? Maybe you learned how to use a new computer. Maybe you learned a new dance movement. Perhaps you learned how to drive a stickshift car. At first the task seemed hard. It felt odd to be doing something you'd never done before. But it got easier each time you did it. The old saying "practice makes perfect" is true. It takes practice to master a new skill.

In this chapter, you will practice the parts of speech you have studied. You will study other parts of speech. You will also practice a four-step writing process.

Goals for Learning

▶ To identify parts of speech in different positions in a sentence

▶ To use owner nouns and pronouns correctly

▶ To use a variety of adverbs

▶ To recognize a sentence with an understood subject

▶ To identify and write interjections

▶ To apply the writing process

Some words in the English language can have more than one part of speech. The part of speech that a word is depends on the use of the word in a sentence.

You have learned about words that can be used as prepositions and adverbs. There also are words that can be used as nouns and verbs. There are words that can be used as nouns and adjectives. There are other words that can be used as nouns, verbs, and adjectives.

EXAMPLES

Adverb:	The woman looked **inside**.
	(*Inside* tells where the woman looked.)
Preposition:	The woman looked **inside** the box.
	(*Inside* introduces the adverb phrase *inside the box*.)
Noun:	Sam starred in the **play**.
	(*Play* is the object of the preposition *in*.)
Verb:	Those boys **play** in a rock band.
	(*Play* is the simple predicate. What do the boys do? They *play*.)
Noun:	This **class** won the contest.
	(*Class* is the subject. Who won? The *class* did.)
Adjective:	Tina ran for **class** president.
	(*Class* describes the noun *president*. It tells what kind of president.)
Noun:	Amy walked through the **park**.
	(*Park* is the object of the preposition *through*.)
Adjective:	Bill and Amy sat on the **park** bench.
	(*Park* describes the noun *bench*. It tells which bench.)
Verb:	Mom will **park** the car in the garage.
	(*Park* is the simple predicate. What will Mom do? She will *park*.)

Activity A Write the part of speech for each word in bold.

 1) Bob and Karen take a long **drive.**

 2) Karen will **drive** during the trip.

 3) Karen will **park** the car near the **park** entrance.

 4) They **walk** in the **park.**

 5) After their **walk**, they stop and sit in the **sun.**

 6) They **sun** themselves on a **park** bench.

 7) Bob thinks about going through the city at **drive** time.

 8) The **farm** lies in a valley.

 9) **Farm** buildings stand near the house.

10) Hugh and his dad **farm** 500 acres along Route 30.

Some forms of verbs can be used as adjectives.

Verb:	The milk **spilled.**
	(*Spilled* is the simple predicate. What happened to the milk? It *spilled*.)
Adjective:	The **spilled** milk ruined my blouse.
	(*Spilled* describes the noun *milk*. It tells which milk.)

Activity B Write the part of speech for each word in bold.

 1) Tom writes a **check** for $100.

 2) The **check** is for the man in the **checked** shirt.

 3) The man will **check** his **watch** and **watch** for Tom.

 4) Tom phoned the man and **checked** in with him.

 5) Dennis **scaled** a fish.

 6) Then he brought the **scaled** fish home.

 7) He weighed the fish on a **scale.**

 8) In the evening, he built a **scale** model of the lake.

Some nouns show ownership. A noun that shows ownership in a sentence is called an **owner noun.** An owner noun may be a proper noun or a common noun.

Use an **apostrophe** plus *s* (*'s*) to form an owner noun that tells about only one owner.

> **Owner noun**
>
> *A noun that owns something in a sentence.*

> **Apostrophe (')**
>
> *A punctuation mark in an owner's name.*

EXAMPLES   **Liz's** long hair falls smoothly.

(Who does the hair belong to? Liz. *Liz* is a proper noun.)

The **child's** toy rolled under the couch.
(Who does the toy belong to? The child. *Child* is a common noun.)

The **tub's** faucet leaks.
(What does the faucet belong to? The tub. *Tub* is a common noun.)

An owner noun may show ownership of a common noun or an abstract noun.

EXAMPLES   We watched the **band's** new video.

(Whose video? The band's. *Video* is a common noun.)

We discussed **Kim's** great ideas.
(Whose ideas? Kim's. *Ideas* is an abstract noun.)

Activity A Write the second sentence in each pair of sentences with an owner noun.

Example   Marian has a family.
              <u>**Marian's**</u> family took her to the movies.

1) Max has a cat.
_____ cat sleeps in the sun.

2) Jake has a car.
_____ car made a wrong turn.

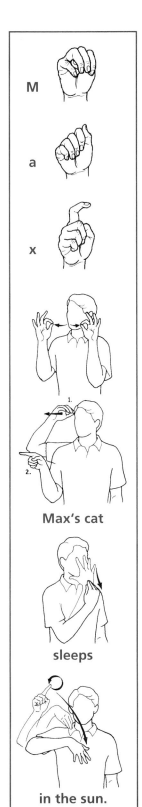

M

a

x

Max's cat

sleeps

in the sun.

3) Henry has a cold.

_____ cold kept him home from work.

4) Megan had a dream.

_____ dream was scary.

5) Kim has a brother.

_____ brother bought a new car.

Activity B Use the information in the box to complete each numbered item below with an owner noun. Write each completed item on your paper.

> The boy has a sleeping bag.
>
> The dog has a bone.
>
> The child has a ball.
>
> The cat has a rubber mouse.
>
> The woman has a bowl of pretzels.
>
> The teenager has some tapes.
>
> The man has a book.
>
> The television has a cord.
>
> The chair has a leg.

When I came home, I tripped on:

Example   the **woman's** bowl of pretzels,

1) the _____ rubber mouse,

2) the _____ ball,

3) the _____ cord,

4) the _____ tapes,

5) the _____ sleeping bag,

6) the _____ bone,

7) the _____ leg, and

8) the _____ book.

Max's cat sleeps in the sun.

You have learned that pronouns can take the place of nouns in a sentence. Pronouns used to show ownership in a sentence are called **owner pronouns.** Owner pronouns do not use apostrophes.

Owner pronoun

A pronoun that owns something in a sentence.

Owner Pronouns	
One Owner	**Two or More Owners**
my	our
your	your
his	their
her	
its	

The noun following the owner pronoun or owner noun is the **owner object.**

Owner object

A noun following an owner pronoun or owner noun.

EXAMPLES   Rita hung **her** coat in the closet.

(The owner pronoun *her* is used in place of the proper noun *Rita. Her* shows that the coat belongs to Rita. *Coat* is the owner object.)

The coin lost **its** value.

(The owner pronoun *its* is used in place of the common noun *coin. Its* shows that the value belongs to the coin. *Value* is the owner object.)

The students left **their** books on the bus.

(The owner pronoun *their* is used in place of the common noun *students. Their* shows that the books belong to the students.)

Activity A Read each sentence. Find all the owner pronouns and write them on your paper. Next to each owner pronoun, write the owner object.

Example   Her brother went around the block on my new bicycle.
Her—brother
my—bicycle

1) Jane and I saw his sister at the movie.

2) Her dog and my cat play in their yard.

3) Your bus, with its orange sign, stops at her house.

4) Our letters arrived at his office.

5) My sweater, your glove, and her scarf are lost.

6) They painted our house and your fence.

7) The man and woman climbed into their old car.

8) Bill had polished his old car carefully.

9) Its left wheel had a flat during their last ride.

10) Their car showed its age.

Activity B Write each sentence. Fill in the blank with an owner pronoun. Look at the list of owner pronouns on page 96 for help.

Example   We visited Neil at the farm and rode on __**his**__ tractor.

1) Lin and I picked berries from _____ garden.

2) We baked a pie, and _____ delicious smell tempted everyone.

3) Mom shared _____ pie-baking secrets with us.

4) Dad gave _____ opinion to the cooks.

5) Jan's brothers washed _____ hands and came to the table.

6) I dropped _____ napkin on the floor.

7) Brad picked up the knife by _____ handle.

8) You forgot _____ coat on the bus.

9) The table has a burn mark on _____ surface.

You have learned that an owner noun can show ownership by one owner. Owner nouns can also show ownership by more than one owner.

Use -*s* apostrophe (*s'*) to form most owner nouns that show ownership by more than one owner.

EXAMPLES

One owner: The woman painted her **daughter's** room.
(One daughter alone has a room.)
More than one owner: The woman painted her **daughters'** room.
(Two or more daughters share the room.)
One owner: The **boy's** tent blew down in the storm.
(One boy alone has a tent.)
More than one owner: The **boys'** tent blew down in the storm.
(Two or more boys share the tent.)

Owner pronouns can also show ownership by more than one owner.

EXAMPLE

More than one owner: The dogs buried **their** bones.

(The owner pronoun *their* shows that the bones belong to more than one dog.)

Activity A   Write each owner's name on your paper.

Example   The birds have songs.   **birds'** songs

1) The kids have toys. _____ toys

2) The parks have paths. _____ paths

3) The horses have saddles. _____ saddles

4) The kittens have milk. _____ milk

5) The trucks have tires. _____ tires

6) The houses have doors. _____ doors

Be careful when using a pronoun to take the place of a noun that names a group such as *team, crowd, army,* and *committee.* Use the pronoun *it* to take the place of a noun that names a group.

EXAMPLE

Group noun: The **pile** of books fell.

Pronoun: **It** fell.

(Although many books fell, only one pile fell.)

Use the owner pronoun *its* to take the place of a group noun that shows ownership.

EXAMPLE

Group noun: The **team's** captain scored a goal.

Pronoun: **Its** captain scored a goal.

(Although there are many players on the team, there is only one team.)

Activity B Write these sentences. Replace the words in bold with pronouns.

1) **A group** sat at the game.

2) **The cheerleaders'** captain began a new cheer.

3) **The team** scored.

4) **A player** grabbed the ball from his opponent.

5) **The crowd** yelled.

6) **The school** won.

Activity C Write these sentences. Replace the words in bold with owner pronouns.

1) **The group's** cheer made the rafters ring.

2) **The school's** score rose after the cheer.

3) **The team's** spirit rose, too.

4) **The crowd's** yells grew.

5) **The band's** music filled the gym.

Every sentence has a subject. Prepositional phrases may make the subject hard to find. Just remember that the object of a preposition is *never* the subject of a sentence.

> **EXAMPLE**
>
> A lot of ice cream melted.
> *adj. noun prep. noun verb*
>
> Parts of speech: *adj. noun prep. noun verb*
> Sentence parts: subject with prep. phrase | predicate
> Sentence pattern: subject + verb

Understood subject

A subject that cannot be seen in a sentence.

Some sentences have **understood subjects.** For example, a sentence spoken to *you* means that *you* are being asked to do something. It is an **understood you.** The subject of the sentence is understood to be *you.*

Understood you

You *as a subject that cannot be seen in a sentence.*

> **EXAMPLE**
>
> Pick up that napkin.
> *verb adv. adj. noun*
>
> Parts of speech: *verb adv. adj. noun*
> Sentence pattern: subject + verb + direct object
> (*You* is the understood subject.)

The subject can be hard to find in sentences where the predicate comes before the subject. These kinds of sentences often begin with the adverbs *here* or *there.* To find the subject in these sentences, try turning the sentence around.

> **EXAMPLES**
>
> There goes the bus.
> *adv. verb adj. noun*
>
> Parts of speech: *adv. verb adj. noun*
> (To find the subject, turn the sentence around.)
> The bus goes there.
> (What goes? The *bus.*)
> Sentence pattern: subject + verb

Activity A Write the subject, verb, and direct object (if there is one) for each sentence. If the subject is understood, write *You.*

1) Bruce earned a lot of money.
2) Come to my house.
3) Take me to work on Tuesday.
4) A lot of money sat on the table.
5) A lot of people wished for the money.
6) Catch that neat action.
7) Watch my bag.
8) Many people want a lot of money.
9) Sit quietly and listen.
10) A lot of trees stand by the road.
11) Read the next chapter by Friday.
12) Look at that paper's ad.
13) A lot of people like Kim.
14) Grab some sleep tonight.
15) Call your parents.
16) Raise your hand.
17) During the game, a lot of batters had hits.
18) Vote for class president.
19) Turn left at Maple Lane.

Activity B Write each sentence so that the subject comes first. Underline the simple subject.

1) Here comes Alice with her friends.
2) Away fly the birds.
3) Here comes the train from New York.
4) There goes the group of children.
5) There lies the problem.

You have learned that adverbs describe verbs. Adverbs can also describe adjectives and other adverbs.

EXAMPLE

The very large ice cream cone melted too fast.

Parts of speech:	*adj.*	*adv.*	*adj.*	*adj.*	*noun*	*verb*	*adv.* *adv.*

Parts of sentence: subject | predicate

(*Very* describes the adjective *large*. *Very* is an adverb. *Too* describes the adverb *fast. Too* is an adverb.)

Try to avoid using *too* and *very* when another adverb will make your sentence more interesting. Here are some adverbs you can use in place of *too* and *very*.

so	almost	completely
quite	rather	unusually
somewhat	really	extremely
truly	terribly	awfully

Activity A Write the adverb in bold in each sentence. Then write the word it describes and its part of speech.

Example   The bus left the corner **very** early.
               very—early, adverb

1) The driver spent **too** many hours on the road.

2) The route covered **extremely** sharp curves.

3) The bus arrived in an **unusually** bad storm.

4) Alan waited a **really** long time for the bus.

5) Snow comes **quite** often in the mountains.

6) It lies **awfully** deep on the roads.

7) Snow and cold weather stay **so** long into the spring.

8) The deep lake freezes **very** slowly.

9) It thaws **rather** quickly in the late spring.

Activity B Choose a word other than *too* or *very* to fill in these blanks. Write the words on your paper.

1) Our _____ snowy winter made a good sports season.

2) Ice and snow made the ski trails _____ slick.

3) Skaters glide _____ fast across the frozen lake.

4) In the evening, people gather by the _____ hot fire at the ski lodge.

5) The _____ cold winter damaged trees and shrubs.

6) Icy ruts made the roads _____ dangerous.

7) Farm animals died during the _____ long winter.

8) Fields of snow glared in the _____ bright sun.

9) _____ strong winds flattened the old barn.

10) _____ long chunks of ice hung from the roof.

11) The _____ chilly fall turned leaves a bright red.

12) _____ large trucks use that road every day.

13) His new car covers the miles _____ quickly.

14) _____ excited students watched the game.

15) _____ hot flames burned logs in the fireplace.

16) Mike's new computer program solves difficult problems _____ fast.

17) The new CD players have _____ good sound.

18) Carla rides _____ fast bikes.

19) Bill always comes _____ late to class.

20) Tristan caused that _____ huge mess.

21) Trina and Jolene watch _____ scary movies.

22) Joy serves _____ tasty pizza.

Interjection
A word that shows strong feelings.

An **interjection** is a word that expresses strong feeling. An interjection often comes first in a sentence.

EXAMPLES   **Oh**, the ice cream melted.

Hey! It's all over the floor.

(*Oh* and *Hey* are both interjections.)

Here are some words that are used as interjections:

hooray	oh	gosh	whoosh
hush	yikes	well	boy
hello	good-bye	yuck	ha
ouch	gee	aha	pow
wow	ah	zap	hey

Activity A Write each sentence. Fill in the blank with an interjection from the list above.

1) _____ ! Jack won a large amount of money.

2) _____ ! The new worker on the night shift works so hard.

3) _____ ! That small airplane landed safely in the dense fog.

4) _____ ! The thick ropes snapped during the daring rescue at sea.

5) _____ ! A black motorcycle roared through the quiet streets.

Activity B Write each sentence. Fill in the blank with an interjection of your choice.

1) _____! Otto's ray gun fired.

2) _____! Otto's ray gun hit Lee's coat.

3) _____! Lee fired his rockets.

4) _____! Lee spun into orbit.

5) _____! Lee fired at Otto.

6) _____! Lee and Otto fell toward Mars.

7) _____! Lee and Otto smashed two holes in the surface.

Do not confuse adverbs that begin a sentence with interjections. Remember, adverbs tell about verbs, adjectives, or other adverbs. Interjections express feelings. They do not tell about any other word in the sentence.

EXAMPLES

Adverb: **Maybe** she solved the problem.

(*Maybe* is an adverb that tells about the verb *solved*. She solved the problem how? *Maybe*.)

Interjection: **Well**, the bus finally arrived.

(*Well* is an interjection that expresses feelings about the arrival of the bus. *Well* does not tell about any other word in the sentence.)

Activity C Write whether the word in bold is an *adverb* or an *interjection*.

1) Hush, the baby is sleeping.

2) Ugh! I really disliked that movie.

3) Perhaps you did not understand it.

4) Maybe Adam left early.

5) Oh, I miss him.

6) Probably he misses you.

7) Aha! We have found the secret passage.

Edit
Checking written work for mistakes.

Prewrite
Talking, thinking, or reading about a topic before writing.

Rewrite
Writing again until the meaning is clear.

Write
Putting ideas on paper.

Writing process
The use of four steps: Prewrite, write, rewrite, and edit.

Writing is a way to express your feelings and ideas. Writing well takes practice. The **writing process** can help you develop good ideas. It can help you focus your thoughts and present them clearly to your readers.

The writing process has four steps: **prewrite, write, rewrite,** and **edit.**

1. **Prewrite.** The first thing you do before writing is decide what you want to write about. Gather your thoughts. Jot them down on paper or note cards. Then arrange your notes so that they make sense.

2. **Write.** Write a first draft, or copy. Write your ideas as clearly as you can, but don't worry about mistakes. You can correct mistakes later.

3. **Rewrite.** You want your writing to express your meaning. Go back and read what you wrote. Can it be improved? Rewrite any sentences that are unclear.

4. **Edit.** Now read your work and look for mistakes in spelling, punctuation, or sentence structure. Be sure to correct all the mistakes you find.

Activity A Read each group of sentences. Then choose one group. Add adverbs, adjectives, compounds, and prepositional phrases to the sentences to write a story. Use the steps of the writing process.

A. 1) Leonard and Regina sit.

   2) Leonard and Regina play chess.

   3) Regina wins the prize.

   4) Regina and Leonard leave.

B. 1) Rachel bakes cookies.

   2) Rachel bakes bread.

   3) Rachel slices bread.

   4) Rachel likes to bake.

   5) Rachel sells baked goods.

C. **1)** Fish swim.

2) Bruce wades.

3) Bruce casts.

4) Bruce reels.

5) Bruce catches fish.

D. **1)** Eddie strolls.

2) Nick walks.

3) Eddie chases.

4) Nick runs.

5) Nick hides.

6) Eddie searches.

7) Nick waits.

E. **1)** Joe gets a shovel.

2) Joe digs.

3) Joe plants.

4) Tree grows.

F. **1)** Oil gushes.

2) Rod yells.

3) Oil stops.

4) Rod stares.

5) Oil starts.

6) Rod gets rich.

G. **1)** Sun shines.

2) Rain falls.

3) Plants grow.

4) Winter comes.

5) Snow falls.

6) Trees and plants sleep.

7) Spring arrives.

You have learned that owner nouns are formed with apostrophes. Use apostrophe and -s to show one owner. Use -s and an apostrophe to show more than one owner.

Activity A Write each sentence correctly on your paper. Don't forget that every sentence begins with a capital letter and ends with a punctuation mark.

1) the mans suit hangs in the closet

2) many trucks tires littered the road

3) frans brother owns a theater

4) four ships sails snapped in the wind

5) a birds nest fell from the branch

6) jans dog really did eat her homework

Interjections that begin a sentence are followed by an exclamation point, a period, or a comma.

An exclamation point is a punctuation mark used when you want to show strong feeling. Use an exclamation point after an interjection that shows strong feelings.

  Yikes! I almost fell down the stairs.
Aha! We caught the thief.

Use a comma after an interjection that shows mild feelings.

  Gee, that movie ended sadly.
Well, we finished our report on time.

Use a period after an interjection to show a pause in thought.

  Oh. I just found your book.
Well. Maybe we should leave now.

Activity B Decide what feeling you want the interjection to show. Then write each sentence correctly.

1) well i found my house

2) ouch you stepped on my foot

3) quick turn on the lights

4) ah i found my shoe

5) oh i fell across the coffee table

6) boom thunder rattled the house

7) crack lightning hit the roof

8) zzzt lightning zapped the stereo the TV and the CD player

9) oh the lightning could have started a fire

10) wow ralph will never forget that terrible night

Activity C Match the words with their meanings. Write the number and its correct letter on your paper.

Words

1) apostrophe

2) interjection

3) owner pronouns

4) sentence pattern

5) exclamation point

Meanings

a) shows feelings

b) !

c) tells word order

d) mark that shows ownership

e) my, his, her, its, your, their

Part A Read this paragraph. Answer the questions on your paper.

> After work, Carlo looks at the used car for sale. The car's doors have dents. The doors' dents aren't bad, though. Carlo's friend bought a car. His car has a dent, too. Gee, Carlo wants this car for work and school.

1) Write the sentence that has an interjection.
2) Write the owner pronoun.
3) Write all the owner nouns with their owner objects. Circle the owner nouns.
4) Find each of these words and tell its part of speech: *After, Carlo, bought, used, and.*

Part B Write these sentences correctly.

5) wow look at that beautiful sunset
6) several spiders webs filled the old barn
7) the red cars door fell off during the race
8) oh my pen ran out of ink
9) now debbies brother plays football
10) the gates old lock broke

Part C Write the part of speech for each word in bold.

11) Adrienne and Julie **talk** to each other by e-mail.
12) One night they had a long **talk** about TV shows.
13) They discussed a **talk** show about rap music.
14) Eric **watched** Jonathan carefully.
15) Jonathan is wearing a new **watch.**
16) Eric is wearing his father's old **watch** cap.
17) Hector **lost** his new pen.
18) The **lost** pen turned up in his jacket pocket.

Part D Write the understood subject, the verb, and the direct object for each sentence.

19) See the new models in the showroom.

20) Grab a hot dog from the grill.

21) Send both boxes to me.

22) Read three books by Monday.

23) Walk the dog every evening.

24) Wow! Feel the beat of the music.

25) Pass the new library on your way home.

26) Stop the car, please.

27) Hang your coat in the closet.

28) Quick! Get a sponge.

Part E Add adverbs, adjectives, compounds, and prepositional phrases to these sentences. Use the writing process to write a story.

29) Cat prowls.

30) Dog walks.

31) Cat runs.

32) Dog chases.

33) Cat turns.

34) Dog barks.

35) Cat hides.

Test Taking Tip Decide which questions you will do first and last. Limit your time on each question accordingly.

Chapter

6

More Sentence Patterns

How would you like it if every day were the same? You would see the same people at the same time and say the same things. You would go to the same places. The weather would be the same. The radio would play the same songs. The world would never change. There would be no surprises. It would get boring very fast.

The same thing is true about writing sentences. You need to use more than one pattern to keep your sentences from being boring.

In this chapter, you will be studying some new sentence patterns. You will learn ways to make your writing more interesting.

Goals for Learning

▶ To identify indirect objects and object complements
▶ To recognize sentences with indirect objects
▶ To identify and write appositives
▶ To identify and write sentences that use different sentence patterns
▶ To use correct punctuation with appositives

Indirect object

A noun or pronoun that takes action from the verb indirectly.

Sentences with direct objects may also have **indirect objects.** An indirect object is a noun or pronoun that takes action from the verb indirectly. An indirect object answers the question *To whom? To What? For Whom?* or *For What?* about the verb.

EXAMPLES

The instructor teaches a lesson.

Parts of speech: adj.   noun   verb adj. noun

Sentence pattern: subject + verb + direct object

The same sentence can have an indirect object.

The instructor teaches **us** a lesson.

Parts of speech: adj.   noun   verb pron. adj. noun

Sentence pattern: subject + verb + indirect object +
                              direct object

(The teacher taught the lesson to whom? To *us. Us* is a pronoun used as an indirect object. *Lesson* is the direct object.)

If you are not sure which word in the sentence is the indirect object, try this: Put *to* or *for* in front of the noun or pronoun. If the sentence still makes sense, the noun is the indirect object.

EXAMPLES   The teacher offered Jon extra help.

Try: The teacher offered extra help **to Jon**.

             Emma saved Tina a seat at the movie.

Try: Emma saved a seat **for Tina** at the movie.

(The sentences makes sense both ways. In the first pair of sentences, *Jon* is the indirect object of the verb *offered. Help* is the direct object. In the second pair of sentences, *Tina* is the indirect object of the verb *saved. Seat* is the direct object.)

Activity A Write the indirect object in each of these sentences. Remember than an indirect object answers the question *To whom? To what? For whom?* or *For what?* about the verb.

1) School gives Alex a pain.

2) Homework gives him trouble.

3) Homework provides students extra practice.

4) The teacher hands Alex a report card.

5) The new semester offers Alex a second chance.

Activity B Write the word in bold. Then write whether it is a *direct object* or *indirect object.*

Example   Jenny bought **Fran** soup and salad.
               Fran—indirect object

1) Mr. Tan paid **Jenny** twenty dollars for mowing his lawn.

2) The clerk handed Jenny the **bill** for lunch.

3) She paid the **clerk** six dollars.

4) The clerk gave her a little **change.**

5) Jenny lent Fran **money.**

6) Fran bought **them** soft drinks.

7) She gave **Jenny** an icy cold bottle of root beer.

8) Jenny's friend told **her** a silly joke.

9) Jenny gave her friend a wide **smile.**

10) Fran's brother Lou offered the girls a **ride** home.

11) His new car gives **him** no problems.

12) Lou showed the **girls** the size of the trunk.

13) They offered him **money** for gas.

14) Jenny gave Lou **directions** to her house.

Sentences with indirect objects may have compound parts and prepositional phrases that add information to the sentence. By identifying the basic parts of the sentence, you can identify the indirect object.

> **EXAMPLE**   The woman and the young girl in the front row of the auditorium asked the speaker on the stage a question at the same time.
>
> Compound subject: woman, girl
> Verb: asked
> Indirect object: speaker
> Direct object: question

Although the example sentence above appears long and complicated, it still follows the basic sentence pattern of *subject + verb + indirect object + direct object*. Eliminate the adjectives and prepositional phrases, and you can easily recognize the sentence pattern.

> **EXAMPLE**   The woman and girl asked the speaker a question.
>
> Sentence pattern: subject + verb + indirect obj. + direct obj.

Activity A   Write the indirect object in these sentences. (HINT: To find the indirect object, first find the verb in each sentence. Then ask *To whom? To what? For whom?* or *For what?* about the verb.)

1) The boy and girl in the back seat of the car told their mom riddles during the long ride home.

2) The frisky little puppy with the red collar brought the young boy on the porch the ball.

3) The radio announcer from WAIL offered listeners of his early morning program a free holiday turkey.

4) Passengers on the flight from Boston to Denver handed the flight attendant at the front of the plane their tickets.

Activity B Write these sentences on your paper. Label the simple subject *S*, the verb *V*, the direct object *DO*, and the indirect object *IO*. Some sentences may have compound parts.

	S	V	IO	DO

Example   Jack drew Emily a picture on a large piece of white paper.

1) The other students in the room asked Jack a question about his picture.

2) Jack taught the group his art style and showed Emily his picture.

3) Some of the students gave Jack a pat on the back for his efforts.

4) Jack gave shy Emily his drawing of her.

5) She sent him her thanks with a smile.

6) Gus and Rose Jackson bought themselves a farm.

7) The Jackson family's hard work on the farm brought them a good life.

8) The children fed the cows hay and corn.

9) The herd of cows gave the family good, rich milk.

10) Gus fed the chickens lots of mash and seed.

11) The hens gave the family dozens of eggs.

12) The oldest daughter fixed the younger children large breakfasts of eggs, bacon, and milk.

13) Rose taught her oldest daughter the farm chores.

14) Rose's work in the city brought the farm more money for repairs.

15) Their son built the animals a new barn with large stalls for the horses.

16) Farm life offered Gus, Rose, and their children joy and profit.

Object complement

A word or words following the direct object that completes the meaning of the verb.

Sentences with direct objects may also have **object complements.** An object complement is an adjective, a noun, or a pronoun that completes the meaning of the verb. An object complement follows the direct object. Like other sentence parts, an object complement may be compound.

An **adjective object complement** follows the direct object and adds meaning to it.

Adjective object complement

An adjective that adds meaning to the direct object.

EXAMPLES   The girl painted the flower **red.**

Sentence parts: *subject   verb   d.obj.   adj. complement*

(The adjective *red* adds meaning to the direct object *flower.* It completes the meaning of the verb by telling what color the girl painted the flower—*red.*)

The rescuers found the hikers **uninjured** and **safe.**

Sentence parts: *subject   verb   d.obj.   adj. complements*

(The adjectives *uninjured* and *safe* add meaning to the direct object *hikers.* It completes the meaning of the verb by explaining how the rescuers found the hikers—*uninjured* and *safe.*)

Noun object complement

A noun that renames the direct object.

A **noun object complement** is a noun or pronoun that follows the direct object and renames it.

EXAMPLES   My brother named the puppy **Ruff.**

Sentence parts: *subject   verb   d.obj.   noun complements*

(The proper noun *Ruff* renames the direct object *puppy.* It completes the meaning of the verb by telling what my brother named the puppy—*Ruff.*)

They consider that problem a minor **one.**

Sentence parts: *subject   verb   d.obj.   adj. complements*

(The pronoun *one* renames the direct object *problem.* It completes the meaning of the verb by explaining how they consider the problem—*a minor one.*)

The girl painted

the flower red.

Activity A Write the adjectives that are object complements in these sentences.

1) Jane likes her soup hot.

2) Most people prefer crackers salty.

3) Sugar makes cereal sweet.

4) Andy likes his onions strong and his coffee weak.

5) Dick serves his salads crisp and his meat rare.

6) Stella painted her car blue and gold.

7) Max liked her car red and white.

8) Willie built his bike low and sleek.

9) Janet wanted her car to be beautiful and fast.

10) She got a car that was rusty and slow.

Activity B Write the nouns or pronouns that are object complements in these sentences.

1) The young man called his old uncle a true friend.

2) The voters in his state elected José senator.

3) Jane called her friends good sports.

4) That movie made the actor a famous person.

5) Many people find the movie an exciting one.

Activity C Fill in the blank with an object complement. Write each completed sentence.

1) Spice makes food _____ .

2) Phil likes his pizza _____ .

3) The man called his friend _____ .

4) Rita named her puppy _____ .

5) Sun turned her skin _____ .

The girl painted the flower red.

Sentences with object complements may have compound parts and prepositional phrases. By identifying the basic parts of the sentence, you can identify the object complement.

> **EXAMPLE** On their honeymoon, the man and his new bride named the rented cottage in the woods beside the lake Our Hideaway.
>
> Compound subject: man, bride
> Verb: named
> Direct object: cottage
> Object complement: Our Hideaway

Although the example sentence has compound parts, adjectives, and adjective phrases, it still follows the basic sentence pattern of *subject + verb + direct object + object complement.* Eliminate the adjectives and prepositional phrases, and you can easily recognize the sentence pattern.

> **EXAMPLE**
>
>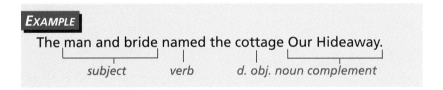
> The man and bride named the cottage Our Hideaway.
> subject   verb   d. obj.   noun complement

Activity A Write the object complement in each sentence. Write whether the complement is an *adjective,* a *noun,* or a *pronoun.*

1) In the moonlight over the water, a bird finds the night a lonely one.

2) At sunset on the pier, a crowd calls the band terrific.

3) By the gate in the park, the girls found a picnic table empty.

4) Down the rutted road through the woods, the driver in the old truck found the road a bumpy mess.

Activity B Make a chart like the one shown. Write the words that form the basic sentence pattern in these sentences in the chart.

Example   Years of work in the fields made the farmer's skin rough and tough.

subject +	verb +	direct object +	object complement
Years	made	skin	rough, tough

1) The new houses and the park made that street a pretty part of town.

2) Lots of training made the dog a good hunter.

3) The quick mechanic kept his tools handy.

4) Some flowering plants need their soil moist.

5) Herds of cattle and horses made the rancher a rich woman.

6) The people in Westown elected Sam Saltz mayor for two years.

7) Hours of work made the finish of the old fire engine shiny.

8) The thirsty scout and his horse found the well water icy cold and refreshing.

Activity C Write whether the word in bold is a *direct object, indirect object, object of a preposition,* or *object complement.*

1) Andy told **him** the final score of the game.

2) Steven quickly passed the news to the **class.**

3) The wonderful news gave the whole class a **thrill.**

4) The boys on the team told their **friends** the news.

5) The news made everyone at school and around town **happy.**

6) The principal declared Friday a **holiday** in honor of the team.

Appositive

A word or group of words that follows a noun and explains the noun or gives another name to the noun.

An **appositive** explains a noun or gives another name to a noun. An appositive may be a single word or a group of words. When an appositive is a group of words, it is usually set off by commas.

EXAMPLES My brother **Luis** works for the city.

(*Luis* is an appositive that gives another name to the noun *brother.*)

Ms. Lee, **the orchestra conductor**, walked on stage.

(*The orchestra conductor* is an appositive that explains who Ms. Lee is. Commas are used to set off the appositive from the rest of the sentence.)

An appositive follows a noun in a sentence. The noun may be the subject, the direct object, the indirect object, or the object of a preposition.

EXAMPLES His friend **Kerry** moved to Japan.

(The appositive *Kerry* renames the subject *friend.*)

The first batter got a hit, **a home run**.

(The appositive *a home run* explains the direct object *hit.*)

Aunt Maria sent my youngest sister **May** a birthday present.

(The appositive *May* renames the indirect object *sister.*)

The children climbed into the back seat of the car, **a station wagon**.

(The appositive *a station wagon* explains *car*, the object of the preposition *of.*)

An appositive may have a prepositional phrase.

EXAMPLE The dessert, **an ice cream sundae with nuts**, melted.

(*An ice cream sundae with nuts* is the appositive. *With nuts* is a prepositional phrase that is part of the appositive.)

Activity A On your paper, write each sentence. Circle the appositive. Underline the noun the appositive explains or renames.

1) The grassy yard, part of a large ranch, glistened in the early morning dew.

2) A barn, the largest building, sits behind the house.

3) Frank, a rancher, gives Joe, the ranch foreman, instructions.

4) A green tractor, one of five, sits near the barn.

5) A fine musician, a trumpet player, played a beautiful song, an old favorite of the crowd.

6) The music, a lively tune, danced in the air.

Activity B Write the appositive in each sentence. Then write whether it names the subject or the direct object.

1) The pirates, a group of thieves, counted their treasure.

2) Big Bart, the leader, buried the huge chest.

3) Bart sailed his boat, a fast ship, into the night.

4) Jenny dug up the chest, a rich prize.

Activity C Add an appositive to each sentence to rename or explain the noun in bold. Write the sentences on your paper. Use commas where needed to set off appositives.

Example   Anna received an invitation to a **party.**

Anna received an invitation to a party, **a surprise birthday celebration for Melissa.**

1) **Anna** went to a wonderful party in the city.

2) She met a tall **boy.**

3) They listened to the music of a great **band.**

4) The **music** was lively and fun.

5) Two dancers demonstrated a new line **dance.**

6) The dancers gave the **crowd** instructions.

7) Anna and Melissa sang a **song** with the band.

Writing is hard but fun. You never know where your thoughts might lead you. You can start with a list of words and end with a story. Another student can begin with the same list of words but write a very different story.

Activity A Using the following list of subjects and direct objects, write nine clear sentences on your paper using action verbs. You may use any subject with any direct object.

Subjects

horse

cat

witch

grandmother

teacher

hero

pitcher

friend

monster

Direct Objects

money

dinner

book

tree

game

grass

television

paper

job

Activity B Using the sentences you wrote in Activity A, add adjectives, adverbs, and prepositional phrases to improve your sentences. Choose from this box, or write your own.

Adjectives		
huge	brave	young
bleak	kind	beautiful
fast	friendly	
old	ugly	

Adverbs		
slowly	loudly	gladly
quickly	quietly	gently
often	wildly	
well	poorly	

Prepositional Phrases	
over the hill	on the chair
to the batter	at the desk
under the table	behind a tree
for a month	in the house
from the fire	around the bend

Activity C Write a story using the list of nouns and appositives below. Before you begin, think about what you want to write. Be sure to use the four-step writing process.

Nouns
Oscar
puppy
Gina

Appositives
dog
a good pet
a lonely girl

Use commas with appositives that are more than one word long. Commas are not usually used with one word appositives, but they may be.

> **EXAMPLES** Jim, **my friend from Ohio,** sent me photographs of his family.
>
> (Commas are needed to set off the long appositive *my friend from Ohio*.)
>
> Correct: My friend **Jim** sent me photographs of his family.
>
> Correct: My friend, **Jim,** sent me photographs of his family.
>
> (Commas are not needed to set off the one-word appositive *Jim*, but they may be used.)

Activity A Write these sentences. Add commas where they are needed. Remember that long appositives need commas.

1) Tony's bike a rocket with wheels roared.

2) Two rabbits scared animals stared into the headlights.

3) They jumped into the ditch a safe place.

4) The moon a beaming light shone on the bikers' helmets.

5) Ann and her best friend Tony rode home together.

Use commas with items in a series. A series is a list of three or more words or phrases connected by a conjunction, such as *and*, *but*, or *or*. Do not put a comma after the last item in a series.

> **EXAMPLES** **Tony, Ann,** and **Chuck** enjoyed their moonlight ride.
>
> (*Tony, Ann,* and *Chuck* are nouns in a series.)
>
> They rode **down the road, over a bridge,** and **through the town** on their journey.
>
> (*Down the road, over a bridge,* and *through the town* are prepositional phrases in a series.)

Activity B Write these sentences correctly. Use commas, periods, exclamation points, and capital letters. You might wish to review what you have learned about writing sentences in previous lessons.

1) wow the batter the teams star hitter knocked the ball over the fence out of the park and down the street

2) down the alley a chill raw winter wind blew

3) bill and senator jacobs visited friends in new york city

4) apples carrots meat and lettuce sat in long cases at the market

5) ms adams mr teeter and dr young sat near the stage at the play

6) bills mother a nice woman had us over for dinner

Activity C Match the words with their meanings. Write the number and its correct letter on your paper.

Words

1) indirect object
2) noun object complement
3) adjective object complement
4) appositive
5) comma

Meanings

a) noun or pronoun that completes a verb's action
b) needed with a long appositive
c) takes action from the verb indirectly
d) adjective that completes a verb's action
e) gives a noun a new name

Part A Write the words in bold in these sentences. Next to each word write its sentence part.

Example   The bank sent our **office** a **check**.
                office—indirect object
                check—direct object

1) A lot of chocolate candy made the **cat sick.**

2) The farmer fed the **pigs** a bushel of **apples.**

3) Some **fishers** like the sky **cloudy.**

4) The pitcher **threw** the catcher a **look.**

5) Jeffrey **mailed Elisha** a package of cookies.

6) Adam likes the kitchen **window open.**

7) **Andrea** gave the **chickens** some water.

8) Years on the **job** at the factory made Dennis **skillful.**

9) The television program left **Patty sad.**

10) Bill **likes** his soup very **hot.**

Part B Read each sentence. Write the letter of the correct sentence pattern.

11) I find this computer game very scary.

12) The small boy plays computer games well.

13) Alex sold him a used computer.

14) The new computer works quietly.

15) That computer program gives me problems.

a) subject + verb

b) subject + verb + direct object

c) subject + verb + indirect object + direct object

d) subject + verb + direct object + object complement

Part C Write each sentence correctly on your paper.

16) the cowboy a thin dude played a tune at the ranch

17) the sky a mass of black clouds closed over the ranch

18) the cook a friendly person greets ranch guests at the door

19) the guests nature lovers hoped for clear weather good for outdoor activities

20) for dinner we ate hamburgers beans and salad in front of a glowing campfire

Part D Use the sentence in parentheses to add an appositive to each sentence. Write the revised sentences on your paper. Use commas where needed.

Example   Ed scored twenty points during the game. (Ed is a fine athlete.)

Ed, **a fine athlete,** scored twenty points during the game.

21) Jenny's computer solved the problem easily. (The computer is a powerful machine.)

22) Tony serves the best lobster in town. (Tony is a great cook.)

23) Black Bilge steered his ship into the harbor. (Black Bilge is an evil pirate.)

24) Greg burned a fast ball to the catcher. (Greg is the best pitcher in the league.)

25) Alex sent three e-mail letters to Holly. (Holly is his best friend.)

Test Taking Tip   When you read test directions, try to restate them in your own words. Tell yourself what you are expected to do. That way, you can make sure your answer will be complete and correct.

Chapter 7

Sentences With Linking Verbs

People have many different sides. Someone you think you know everything about may suddenly reveal a hidden talent or skill. Even best friends can surprise you by showing new sides to their personality. The more sides a person has, the more interesting that person becomes.

Sentences are like that, too. Some sentences tell more than one fact about a subject. Words in the predicate can give new names to the subject or describe it.

In this chapter, you will study more about sentences and new ways they can give information.

Goals for Learning

▶ To identify linking verbs and sentence patterns that use them

▶ To identify and use subject complements in sentences

▶ To use comparative and superlative adjectives correctly

▶ To use *good* and *well* correctly

Subject complement

A word in the predicate that describes the subject.

Noun subject complement

A noun or pronoun in the predicate that renames the subject.

Linking verb

A verb that connects the subject to a word in the predicate.

Subject complements describe the subject of a sentence. **Noun subject complements** are words in the predicate that give a new name to the subject. Remember that a sentence has two parts: the subject and the predicate. A noun (or pronoun) in the predicate may rename the subject. A **linking verb** links the predicate with the subject.

EXAMPLE   This cereal is a fat-free brand.

Parts of sentence: subject | predicate

Sentence pattern: subject + linking verb + noun subject complement

(The linking verb *is* in this sentence links the subject *cereal* with a noun in the predicate *brand. A fat-free brand* is the noun subject complement.)

Activity A Write the subject in each sentence. Then write the noun in the predicate that is linked to the subject by the linking verb. The linking verb is in bold.

Example   That super movie star **is** my hero.
                 star—hero

1) Tennis **is** your favorite game.

2) Football **is** my best sport.

3) Lincoln and Kennedy **were** presidents.

4) Laura **is** a speedy worker.

5) Her friend **is** a helpful person.

6) A ski trip **is** the first prize.

7) Sam and Gary **are** fast runners.

8) Patty and David **are** neighbors.

9) James **is** a very good student.

Activity B Write the complete noun subject complement in each sentence. The linking verb in each sentence is in bold.

Example   Bruce Willis **is** a busy actor.
a busy actor

1) Many of his movies **are** exciting adventures.

2) He **is** a popular movie star.

3) Most of his movies **are** box office hits.

4) My friends and I **are** loyal fans.

5) Craig **is** the band's leader.

6) This band **is** a good one.

7) Their music **is** a fine choice.

8) Pat, Jenny, and Christa **are** marchers.

9) Victor **is** a drummer.

10) The school band **is** a talented group.

11) A thick novel **is** a vacation treat.

12) The plot of this book **is** an exciting one.

13) The book's hero **was** a doctor.

14) Her friends **were** scientists.

15) Their enemy **was** fever.

16) Their job **was** a hard one.

17) A new medicine **was** their discovery.

18) Their victory **was** a breakthrough.

Activity C Complete each of these sentences with a noun subject complement. Write the sentences on your paper.

1) Their trip to Africa was _____ .

2) My aunt and uncle are _____ .

3) That story is _____ .

4) Good friends are _____ .

5) The cat and dog were _____ .

You have learned three ways that a noun or a pronoun can give a new name to another noun in the sentence. Notice the different ways that the noun *dessert* is renamed in each of the following examples.

EXAMPLE

Noun object complement:	I made the dessert a big **one**.
Appositive:	The dessert, an ice cream **cake**, melted.
Noun subject complement:	The dessert was a refreshing **treat**.

Sometimes a noun in the subject can be renamed in more than one place in a sentence.

EXAMPLE The magician, a clever man, is an amazing person.

        subject   *appositive*   *noun subject complement*

(The subject noun *magician* is renamed twice: first, by the noun *man* in the appositive *a clever man*; and second, by the noun *person* in the noun subject complement *an amazing person*.)

Activity A On your paper, write each noun in bold. Next to each noun, write the noun or nouns that rename it.

1) **Jack** and **Helen,** our new neighbors, are a busy couple.

2) The **coach,** a happy guy, is also our teacher and friend.

3) The country **man,** a shy person, found the city a noisy place.

4) The **library,** a room full of books, was a quiet place.

5) My **boss,** an organized woman, straightened out her office, a large, bright room.

6) Those two young **men,** clerks at the store, are helpful people.

You can write sentences with appositives and subject complements. Follow these steps:

1. Identify the parts of the sentence.
   Subject: girl
   Appositive: student
   Subject complement: writer

2. Write the sentence. Use the linking verb *is* or *was*.
   The girl, a student, is a writer.

3. Add adjectives to describe the nouns.
   The quiet girl, a bright student, is a good writer.

Activity B Use each group of words to write a sentence with an appositive and a subject complement. Follow the steps described above.

1) cat, pet, friend
2) woman, singer, dancer
3) building, house, home
4) dog, puppy, animal
5) skater, athlete, winner
6) man, worker, carpenter
7) woman, neighbor, pilot
8) parrot, bird, pet
9) sundae, dessert, treat
10) actor, star, performer
11) house, home, place
12) car, beauty, racer
13) book, favorite, thriller
14) CD, winner, music
15) airplane, jet, flyer
16) friend, doctor, person

An adjective in the predicate of a sentence may describe the subject noun. The adjective and any words that describe that adjective make up the **adjective subject complement.**

Adjective subject complement

A word in the predicate that describes the subject.

EXAMPLE   This cereal is fat-free.

Parts of speech: *adj. noun verb adj.*

Sentence pattern: subject + linking verb + adjective subject complement

(The linking verb *is* links the subject noun *cereal* to the adjective in the predicate *fat-free*. *Fat-free* is the adjective subject complement.)

An adjective subject complement always follows a linking verb. Remember that a linking verb connects the predicate with the subject.

Here is a list of linking verbs:

be	are	grow	feel
being	were	appear	smell
been	am	seem	look
is	was	taste	sound

Activity A Write the adjective subject complement in each sentence.

1) These two good friends are close.

2) Their clothes are old and worn.

3) Their pockets and stomachs are empty.

4) Their travels were exciting.

5) Their smiles are warm and friendly.

6) Their friendship is true.

Activity B Write these sentences on your paper. Underline the linking verb in each sentence. Draw an arrow from the adjective subject complement to the subject in bold.

Example The **food** at that diner <u>tastes</u> delicious.

1) Their fresh **vegetables** are terrific.
2) The **pies** look great.
3) The **coffee** smells wonderful.
4) Each **customer** seems happy.
5) That dark **alley** seems long.
6) Every **shadow** looks scary.
7) **Piles** of garbage smell awful.
8) The **air** feels damp.
9) Distant **lights** appear dim.

Activity C Complete each sentence with an adjective subject complement. Write the sentences on your paper.

1) The city is _____ .
2) The crowded streets are _____ .
3) City people are _____ .
4) City lights are _____ .
5) City life is _____ .
6) The country seems _____ .
7) The farms appear _____ .
8) The breeze feels _____ .
9) The mountains look _____ .
10) The country food tastes _____ .

An adjective always describes a noun in a sentence. Most adjectives come right before the nouns they describe. An adjective may, however, follow the noun it describes or be separated from the noun by a linking verb.

Notice the placement of the adjectives that describe the noun *bear* in these sentences.

EXAMPLE

Adjectives before a noun:	The **hungry, brown** bear growled.
Adjective object complement:	Someone called the bear **large**.
Adjective subject complement:	To me, the bear seemed **huge**.

A noun may be described by more than one adjective. These adjectives may come before and after the noun.

EXAMPLE   I find the **young** magician **clever**.

(The adjectives *young* and *clever* both describe the noun *magician*. *Clever* is an adjective object complement.)

Activity A Write the adjectives that describe the nouns in bold in these sentences.

1) Tasha finds large **cities** fun.

2) The long **streets** are busy.

3) Night makes the big **city** exciting.

4) She finds the bright **lights** pretty.

5) In the morning, the sun makes the tall, glass **buildings** shiny.

6) Tony, the cook, makes good **food** great.

7) He makes the beef **stew** spicy.

8) The fresh, green **vegetables** are crisp.

9) He serves the sparkling **water** cold.

To me,

the bear

seemed huge.

You can write sentences with adjectives like those in Activity A. Follow these steps:

1. Choose a noun.
   Noun: man

2. Choose two or more adjectives to describe the noun.
   Adjectives: young, bright

3. Decide on a sentence pattern and write the sentence.
   a. subject + verb + d. object + adj. obj. complement
   Sharon called the young man bright.
   b. subject + linking verb + adj. subj. complement
   The young man is bright.

Activity B Write a sentence for each group of words. Use an adjective object complement in seven sentences (pattern *a* above). Use an adjective subject complement in the other seven sentences (pattern *b* above).

1) ice cream cone, soft, cold
2) sun, bright, shiny
3) woman, careful, busy
4) car, old, broken
5) soccer player, active, quick
6) elephant, trained, strong
7) prison, dark, scary
8) cat, fussy, hungry
9) boat, wooden, leaky
10) bike, loud, fast
11) flower, bright, pretty
12) student, smart, eager
13) alley, narrow, dirty
14) coffee, hot, black

To me, the bear seemed huge.

Some adjectives become adverbs when *-ly* is added.

EXAMPLES

Adjectives: quiet, soft, quick, noisy

Adverbs: quietly, softly, quickly, noisily

To figure out whether a word is an adjective or an adverb, look carefully at the whole sentence.

- If the word comes right before a noun or if it follows a linking verb, it is probably an adjective.

- If the word ends in *-ly* and follows an action verb, it is probably an adverb.

Remember that an adjective always describes a noun. An adverb tells about a verb, an adjective, or another adverb.

EXAMPLES   Adjective: The boy seems **active**.

(The linking verb *seems* links the adjective *active* to the noun *boy*. *Active* is an adjective subject complement.)

Adverb: The boy plays **actively**.

(The adverb *actively* answers the question *How?* about the action verb *plays*.)

Activity A On your paper, write whether the word in bold is an *adjective* or *adverb*. (You may wish to refer to the list of linking verbs in Lesson 3 on page 136.)

1) The birds in the park appeared **happy.**

2) The birds sang **happily.**

3) It was a **happy** day for everyone.

4) The winter wind felt **brisk** and cold.

5) Mr. Stillman walked **briskly** to his car.

Activity B Write the word in parentheses that completes each of these sentences correctly. Next to the word, write whether it is an *adjective* or *adverb*.

Example   Al stacked papers in a (neat, neatly) pile.
              neat—adjective

  1) The (heavy, heavily) load shifted.

  2) The load fell (heavy, heavily) to the street.

  3) (Quick, Quickly), the papers blew along the curb.

  4) The boat moved (slow, slowly) out of the harbor.

  5) The skipper handled the sailboat (careful, carefully).

  6) Then a (strong, strongly) south wind moved the boat along (swift, swiftly).

  7) The wind blew (awful, awfully) hard on that (terrible, terribly) stormy day.

The adjective *good* and the adverb *well* are often used incorrectly.

- Use *good* after a linking verb to describe the subject. Always use *good* to describe a noun or pronoun.

- Use *well* after an action verb to tell about the verb.

EXAMPLES	Adjective:	That meal was **good**.
		We ate a **good** lunch.
	Adverb:	They ate **well** after their hike.

Activity C Write *good* or *well* to complete each sentence correctly.

  1) That dress looks _____ on her.

  2) She slept _____ during the storm.

  3) The old house is in _____ shape.

  4) A cold drink tastes _____ on a hot day.

  5) Vic works _____ under pressure.

  6) Kay's friends are _____ people.

Sentences with subject complements may have compound parts and prepositional phrases. Two or more subject complements make a **compound subject complement.**

Compound subject complement

Two or more subject complements joined by a conjunction.

> **EXAMPLE**   On a hot summer day, chocolate candy and melted suckers in a warm car are **messy, sticky, and runny.**
>
> Compound subject: candy, suckers
> Linking verb: are
> Compound subject complement: messy, sticky, runny

Although the example sentence has compound parts, adjectives, and prepositional phrases, it still follows the basic sentence pattern of *subject + linking verb + subject complement.* Eliminate the adjectives and prepositional phrases, and you can easily recognize the sentence pattern.

> **EXAMPLE**
>
> Candy and suckers are messy, sticky, and runny.
>
> compound subject   verb   compound subject complement

Activity A Write the subject complement in each sentence. Write whether the complement is a *noun subject complement* or an *adjective subject complement.*

1) Of all the town's cooks, Juan is the most talented chef.
2) For meats, Juan's own gravy recipe is a great one.
3) Over steaming rice, Juan's pepper beef stew with gravy and vegetables tastes spicy and terrific.
4) For a side dish, Juan's salads of mixed greens are extremely fresh and tasty.
5) On Friday nights, Juan's restaurant in the city is full of happy diners.
6) Without a doubt, diners at Juan's place are completely satisfied customers.

Activity B Make a chart like the one shown. Write the words that form the basic sentence pattern in these sentences in the chart.

Example The woman with top honors in law school became a lawyer and then a judge within a few years.

subject + linking verb + subject complement		
woman	became	lawyer, judge

1) Most of the stores in town are bargain shops with good values at low cost.

2) Gina's friends are natives of the northern part of the state.

3) The price of that blue coat in the store on Elm Street looks good to me.

4) The bus with the red sign was late on its way to the station.

5) Lisa, a healthy, young student, was an active member of the Hikers Club and an experienced skier.

6) The fine athlete is a major player on the team and an excellent student at his school in New York.

7) My brand-new computer is a wonderful machine and a useful tool for almost any job.

Activity C Add adjectives, adverbs, compounds, and prepositional phrases to each sentence. Write the sentences on your paper.

1) Josh's car is a wreck.

2) The hood is dented.

3) Two windows are broken.

4) The tires appear flat.

5) Josh's ribs are bruised.

6) His pockets are empty.

7) That boy is one unhappy person.

Pronouns are often used as subjects of sentences with linking verbs. Examples of pronouns used as subjects with linking verbs are:

it	that	those
this	these	

EXAMPLE This is a new book by your favorite writer.

Sentence pattern: subject + linking verb + subject complement

(The pronoun *this* is the subject of the sentence.)

Activity A Write each sentence on your paper. Write *S* above the subject pronoun, *LV* above the linking verb, and *NSC* above the noun subject complement.

Example
          S   LV   NSC
          Those were the best cows in the herd.

1) This is the time for the picnic.

2) That is the dog with the sore foot.

3) These are the hottest months of the year.

4) It was a neat deal.

5) This is a sea turtle from Florida.

6) It is an animal in trouble.

7) That is a very common problem.

8) That was our last chance for help.

The adverbs *here* and *there* often appear first in sentences with linking verbs. To find the subject in sentences that begin with *here* or *there*, try turning the sentence around so that the noun or pronoun subject comes before the verb.

EXAMPLE

Here is the morning paper.

There is the express bus.

Parts of speech: adv. verb adj. adj. noun

To find the subjects, reverse the word order.

The morning paper is here.

The express bus is there.

Sentence pattern: subject + verb

(The subject of the first sentence is *paper*. The subject of the second sentence is *bus*. The sentence pattern of the original sentences is *subject + verb* even though the order of the words is reversed.)

Activity B Write the subject of each sentence. If you have trouble finding the subject, try turning the sentence around. Two sentences have a compound subject.

1) There is a sailboat at the end of the lake.

2) Here is the key to the old chest.

3) There is a low, black car on the hilly road.

4) There is a herd of cattle and some sheep on the grassy hill.

5) There was a campfire near the lake.

6) There were bright flashes of lightning and loud cracks of thunder during the storm.

7) Here is a hot cup of coffee.

8) Here are the movie tickets to the next show.

9) There is a silver jet on the runway.

10) There was a moving van in front of his house.

You have learned that pronouns can take the place of nouns in a sentence.

Pronouns			
	Nominative	**Objective**	**Owner**
One	I	me	my, mine
	you	you	you, yours
	he, she, it	him, her, it	his, her, hers, its
Two or	we	us	our, ours
More	you	you	your, yours
	they	them	their, theirs

Nominative pronouns are used as subjects and as subject complements in sentences with linking verbs. Objective pronouns are used as direct objects and indirect objects in sentences with action verbs and as objects of prepositions.

EXAMPLES	Subject:	I am happy.
	Subject complement:	It is **I**.
	Direct object:	Jim saw **me**.
	Indirect object:	Jim gave **me** a pen.
	Object of preposition:	Jim gave a pen to **me**.

Owner pronouns are often used as subject complements in sentences with linking verbs. These owner pronouns are:

mine	yours	his	hers	its	ours	theirs

EXAMPLE

That book is **his**.

Parts of speech: *adj.* *noun* *verb pronoun*

Parts of sentence: subject | predicate

Sentence pattern: subject + linking verb + subject complement

Activity A Write the correct pronoun in parentheses. Then write how each pronoun is used in the sentence.

Example   Ed gave (he, him) and (I, me) tickets to the play.
him, me—compound indirect object

1) (He, Him) and (I, me) sat together during the show.

2) Tony met (he, him) and (she, her) after the play.

3) The four of (we, us) ate at Jake's.

4) (He, Him) and (I, me) liked the play, but Cora did not.

5) The best tennis players are (he, him) and (she, her).

6) (Her, She) slams the ball across the net to (him, he).

7) The winners of the match are (they, them).

8) Afterward, (he, him) asked (she, her) for a ride home.

9) The waiter served lunch to (he, him) and (she, her).

10) The person in the picture is (she, her).

Activity B On your paper, write the second sentence of each set. Fill in the blank with an owner pronoun.

Examples   Those papers belong to me.
They are __**mine**__ .

1) Those clothes belong to Brigette.
They are _____ .

2) Mr. and Mrs. Lee own the store.
It is _____ .

3) That car belongs to Rob.
It is _____ .

4) The books belong to you.
They are _____ .

5) We own the table.
It is _____ .

6) I own the bike.
It is _____ .

Remember, there are six sentence patterns.

1. Subject + verb
Ice cream melts.

2. Subject + verb + direct object
The ice cream stained the cloth.

3. Subject + verb + indirect object + direct object
He served her an ice cream sundae.

4. Subject + verb + direct object + object complement
I find this ice cream messy.

5. Subject + linking verb + noun subject complement
This ice cream is a fat-free brand.

6. Subject + linking verb + adjective subject complement
The ice cream sundae is big.

Activity A Identify the correct sentence pattern for each sentence. Write the number that matches one of the sentence patterns above.

Example   The class of English students opened their books to the chapter on nouns.

        2 (subject + verb + direct object)

1) Todd was late again.

2) The late student dashed in with a pile of books and gave the teacher his homework.

3) Ms. Costa turned to the class and asked the students a question.

4) Steven gave the right answer.

5) Steven felt smart, and he was proud of himself.

6) He smiled happily.

7) Then she taught the class another grammar lesson.

8) Ms. Costa is a good English teacher.

9) Most students thought the lesson an easy one.

10) Several began their work.

11) Ms. Costa allowed them ten minutes.

12) Everyone finished on time.

13) Well, Todd was a little slow with his paper.

14) Later, the teacher corrected the papers quickly.

15) After school, Troy offered Gina a ride home.

16) Troy's old car is a rare model.

17) The car is long and green.

18) The tires are white.

19) Those tires are a special brand.

20) Most people call the car sharp.

21) A few call it fast.

22) Troy is proud of his car.

23) He washes the car every week.

24) He waxes the car every month.

25) He changes the oil often.

26) He tunes the engine monthly.

27) He finds the work fun.

28) Troy showed his friend the car.

29) She offered him cash for the car.

30) He turned down her offer.

31) That car is too special.

32) Troy will keep his car.

Activity B On your paper, write a new sentence for each of the six sentence patterns.

You know that a sentence is a group of words arranged in a certain pattern to express an idea. You and a friend may start with the same list of words, but you will probably write totally different sentences that express different ideas. Your choice of words and how you arrange them will create a different picture in a reader's mind than your friend's sentence will.

Look at the following list of words. Think about an idea for a sentence using some of these words. Then compare your idea with the sentences that other students wrote.

Subjects	Adjectives	Subject Complements
day	bright	gloomy
night	dark	one
	new	
	starry	
	lovely	

Here are other students' sentences:

The new, bright day was gloomy in the afternoon.

The bright, starry night was a lovely one.

Activity A Use this list of subjects, adjectives, and subject complements to write five clear sentences using linking verbs. Add other words as needed.

Subjects	Adjectives	Noun and Adjective Subject Complements
pizza	thick	cheap
steak	greasy	one
salad	hot	food
coffee	crispy	great
fruit	juicy	treat

Activity B Improve the sentences you wrote in Activity A by adding adverbs and prepositional phrases. Write your revised sentences on your paper.

Activity C Use the sentences from Activity B to write a story about food. Proofread and edit your story.

Activity D Use this list of subjects, adjectives, and subject complements to write five clear sentences using linking verbs. Add other adjectives as needed.

Subjects	Adjectives	Noun and Adjective Subject Complements
lion	cute	angry
bear	hairy	animal
wolf	scary	creature
snake	toothy	noisy
monkey	strong	huge

Activity E Improve the sentences you wrote in Activity D by adding adverbs and prepositional phrases. Write your revised sentences on your paper.

Activity F Use the sentences from Activity E to write a story about zoo animals. Proofread and edit your story.

Activity G Now it's your turn. Think about a topic: for example, cars, sports, movies, music, computer games, or anything that interests you. Next, make a list of words that you might use to describe your topic. You might wish to list the words in a chart similar to the charts shown in this lesson. Finally, follow the steps in the writing process to write a story on your topic.

Comparative

An adjective that compares two nouns.

Superlative

An adjective that compares three or more nouns.

Adjectives compare people, places, and things. When two things are being compared, the adjective usually has an *-er* added to it. Adjectives that compare two things are called **comparatives.** When more than two things are being compared, the adjective usually has an *-est* added to it. Adjectives that compare more than two things are called **superlatives.**

EXAMPLES

Sue is:	Of the two, Kim is:	Of the three, Pam is:
quick	quicker	quickest
tall	taller	tallest
early	earlier	earliest
hungry	hungrier	hungriest
happy	happier	happiest

Some adjectives change completely to form their comparative and superlative forms.

EXAMPLES

Adjective	Comparative	Superlative
bad	worse	worst
good	better	best
little	less	least
many	more	most

Activity A On your paper, write the correct form of the adjective in parentheses for each sentence.

1) Todd is the (faster, fastest) runner on the whole team.

2) Of the two comics, she is the (funnier, funniest).

3) Henry is the (fatter, fattest) cat on the block.

4) The Empire State Building was once the (taller, tallest) building in the world.

5) Maria is the (older, oldest) of the two sisters.

Activity B Write the correct form of the adjective in parentheses for each sentence.

1) Of the mother and daughter, the daughter is (tallest, taller).

2) The pig is the (smarter, smartest) of all the animals in that story.

3) This winter was cold, but last winter was the (colder, coldest) in ten years.

4) My test scores are high, but Jeff's are (higher, highest).

5) Ted's computer is fast, but Cathy's computer is (fast, faster).

6) Of the three recipes, Jean's bread dough is (higher, highest).

7) Of the two loaves, this bread is (tastier, tastiest).

8) That store carries the (fresher, freshest) vegetables of any store in town.

9) Our house has the (fewer, fewest) windows on the block.

Activity C Write the correct form of the adjective in parentheses for each sentence.

1) Many people find her the (more, most) talented of all stage actors.

2) In all the family, she is (more, most) famous.

3) Of the two sisters, her acting is (better, best).

4) Her singing is (worse, bad), but she has the (best, better) voice of all the sisters.

5) Of the two problems, this is (less, least) difficult.

6) It is my (least, less) favorite of all.

7) My grades are (good, better), but yours are (best, better).

8) Of the five team members, Pauline has scored the (more, most) points.

9) The Blue Devils had a bad season, but the Blazers had the (worse, worst) record in the league.

10) Of the two teams, their record is (worse, worst).

Part A Read this paragraph.

> Josh's truck is good for long trips. His truck carries heavy loads. Two of Josh's friends are his partners. He and they split the costs of each trip. Truck travel pays well for him and them. Josh feels proud of his truck.

Find these words in the paragraph. Match them with the correct labels. On your paper, write the numbers and letters.

Words

1) He
2) partners
3) well
4) feels
5) good
6) him

Labels

a) linking verb
b) adjective subject complement
c) pronoun as a subject
d) pronoun as an object of a preposition
e) noun subject complement
f) adverb

Part B Write the correct adjective in parentheses for each sentence.

7) Of the three men, Josh is the (better, best) driver.

8) Josh drove on the (better, best) of the two roads.

9) The city's freeway is the (busier, busiest) of all its roads.

10) Rush hour is the (worse, worst) time of day for traffic.

11) This is the (quicker, quickest) of all the routes to town.

12) That street has (bad, worse) potholes, but the potholes on this street are (worse, worst).

Part C Write the correct adjective in parentheses for each sentence.

13) Choose (good, well) words and use them (good, well).

14) Ray did very (good, well) on his last exam.

15) Sam and Jean work (good, well) together.

16) During the night, the wind blew (real, really) hard.

17) The team seems (happy, happily) about the new coach.

18) Gloria's old car is in (good, well) shape.

19) Jason's team won the trophy (easy, easily).

20) Mary uses her study time (good, well).

Part D Write the sentence pattern for each of these sentences. Look back at the list of sentence patterns and example sentences in Lesson 9 on page 148 for help.

21) They solved all our problems.

22) His dogs are healthy.

23) Hockey is my favorite game.

24) The students seem happy.

25) Terry and Marge are good friends.

26) That singer is a big name.

27) Jody and Beth found that video boring.

28) Patrick bought her a ticket to the rodeo.

29) George ran the ball into the end zone.

30) Birds land on a tree branch under my window.

Test Taking Tip

When you don't know the answer to a question, put a check beside it and go on. After you finish the test, go back to the checked questions. Try again to answer them.

8

Verbs Tell Time

How do you know what time it is when you don't have a watch? You might try to guess how much time has passed since you last looked at a clock. If it's a sunny day, you might look at the location of the sun in the sky. If you feel hungry, you might assume that it's mealtime. You can use a variety of clues to estimate time.

Sentences give clues about time, too. They tell if an event happened in the past, if it's happening now, or if it will happen tomorrow or some other time in the future. The verb in a sentence tells you if the time is in the past, present, or future.

In this chapter, you will practice using verbs in sentences to tell when things happened.

Goals for Learning

▶ To use verbs in past, present, and future forms

▶ To use helping verbs and negative adverbs

▶ To use correct forms of irregular verbs

▶ To identify and use contractions

Verbs show action or a state-of-being. An action verb tells what the subject of a sentence is doing. Linking, or state-of-being, verbs link the subject to nouns or adjectives in the predicate. Linking verbs help the predicate tell more about the subject.

Activity A Write the verb in each sentence. Next to each verb, write whether it is an *action verb* or a *linking verb*.

1) The wet streets shine under the light.

2) Ron works the late shift.

3) He seems really sick today.

4) Andy feels awful, too.

5) His cold is pretty bad.

6) Both men left work early.

In a sentence, the verb is the word that tells you the time something happens. **Tense** refers to the time expressed by the verb. The tense of a verb tells you whether something:

- happened in the past

- is happening in the present, or

- will happen in the future

Regular verbs form their past tense by adding *-d* or *-ed* at the end. Add *-d* to regular verbs that end in *-e*. Add *-ed* to regular verbs that end in other letters.

Tense

Present, past, or future time expressed by a verb.

Regular verb

A verb that adds -d or -ed to form the past tense.

EXAMPLES		
Present:	Today, I **smile**.	
Past:	Yesterday, I **smiled**.	
Future:	Tomorrow, I **will smile**.	
Present:	Today, I **walk**.	
Past:	Yesterday, I **walked**.	
Future:	Tomorrow, I **will walk**.	

Activity B Write the verbs in these sentences. (Include the word *will* with future tense verbs.) Write whether the verb is in the *present, past,* or *future tense.*

1) Yesterday, I changed schools.

2) Today, I talk with my teacher.

3) Yesterday, I started class.

4) Tomorrow, I will learn about verbs.

5) Yesterday, I learned about sentences.

6) Yesterday, I jumped rope.

7) Tomorrow, I will play basketball with my friends.

8) Today, I watch TV at home.

9) Yesterday, you looked sad about something.

10) Today, you appear fine.

Activity C Complete each sentence with the bold verb and the tense in parentheses. Write the sentence on your paper. Each of the verbs given is a regular verb.

Example   Those bells _____ louder than usual.
(**sound,** past tense)
Those bells **sounded** louder than usual.

1) Lin _____ quite happy about her test grade.
(**seem,** past tense)

2) The pizza _____ quite spicy. (**taste,** past tense)

3) The girls _____ about their plans for the summer. (**talk,** future tense)

4) I _____ for a happy ending to the story.
(**wish,** past tense)

5) She _____ the steps for the directions in order. (**list,** future tense)

6) Roberto and Joey _____ to the train station.
(**rush,** present tense)

7) He _____ his report on the computer.
(**revise,** past tense)

8) I _____ the school computer for research.
(**use,** future tense)

Helping verb

A verb that comes before the main verb. Together, the two verbs form a verb phrase.

A **helping verb** is a verb that comes before the main verb. A helping verb *helps* the main verb show action or state a fact. A main verb with one or more helping verbs is a **verb phrase.**

EXAMPLES   I **was dreaming.**

He **could be dreaming.**

You **must have been dreaming.**

(In each of the verb phrases, *dreaming* is the main verb. *Was, could, be, must, have,* and *been* are all helping verbs.)

Verb phrase

A verb and its helpers.

Forms of the verbs *be, have,* and *do* are often used as helping verbs. They are included in this list of common helping verbs:

am	is	having	did	shall
are	was	had	can	should
be	were	do	could	may
been	has	does	would	might
being	have	doing	will	must

Verbs in the future tense always use a helping verb.

EXAMPLE   Ann **will go** to the store later.

(The verb phrase *will go* is made up of the main verb *go* and the helping verb *will*.)

Activity A Write the bold verb phrase in each sentence. Draw one line under the main verb. Circle the helping verbs.

1) Hannah **has packed** her bags.

2) She **will be leaving** tomorrow.

3) Hannah and her friends **are going** on a trip.

4) They **have been looking** forward to this vacation.

5) Kerry **did plan** all of their stops on the way.

Activity B Write the verb phrase in each sentence. Draw one line under the main verb. Circle the helping verbs.

  1) Jake will earn extra money at his job.

  2) Then he can buy a Mother's Day gift.

  3) The store does deliver gifts for its best customers.

  4) The gift should surprise Jake's mother.

  5) Probably she will be smiling happily all day.

  6) Pamela did go to the dentist.

  7) Her brother must visit the dentist, too.

  8) They could have been checked at the same time.

  9) Pamela has been taking good care of her teeth.

10) The dentist will praise her.

Activity C Complete each sentence with a verb phrase. Use the verb in parentheses and one or more helping verbs from the list on page 160. Write the completed sentences on your paper.

Example   Ted, a grain and cattle farmer, _____ hard. (work)

Ted, a grain and cattle farmer, **has been working** hard.

1) He _____ many acres of corn. (plant)

2) He _____ his corn in that tall silo. (store)

3) He _____ some of his corn to his cattle. (feed)

4) Ted _____ his fields carefully. (tend)

5) She _____ the most beautiful quilt all by hand. (stitch)

6) Luisa _____ her quilt at the fair. (show)

7) She _____ it in the craft contest. (enter)

8) Her quilt _____ the first prize. (award)

Present tense

The tense of verbs that tells about action in the present.

Verbs that tell about action that takes place now or continues to take place are in the **present tense.** There are four present tense verb forms.

EXAMPLES

Natalie **plays** basketball.

Natalie **is playing** on a team.

Natalie **has played** well all season.

Natalie **has been playing** basketball for three years.

The helping verbs for present tense are *am, is, are, have, has, has been,* and *have been.*

EXAMPLES

I **am running**.	You **have run**.
He **is running**.	She **has run**.
They **are running**.	We **have been running**.

Activity A Number your paper from 1 to 4. Rewrite the following sentence four times. Each time, use a different form of the present tense for the verb *wait*.

Susie, the cat, _____ for a mouse.

Verbs must agree with their subjects. Many verbs add an *-s* or *-es* to their present tense form when the subject of a sentence is singular.

EXAMPLES

| Singular subject: | Ed **looks**. | He **watches**. |
| Plural subject: | Ed and Joe **look**. | They **watch**. |

In sentences with verb phrases, the helping verbs must agree with the subjects.

EXAMPLES

| Singular subject: | Pam **does** look. | He **is** watching. |
| Plural subject: | I **do** look. | We **are** watching. |

- Never use *be* as a helping verb in present tense verbs.
- Never use *been* alone as a helping verb or as a main verb.
- Use *has* or *have* with *been*.

> **EXAMPLES**   Incorrect: They **be** waiting for a bus.
> Correct: They **are waiting** for a bus.
> Incorrect: They **been waiting** for an hour.
> Correct: They **have been waiting** for an hour.

Activity B Write these sentences using the correct present tense forms of the verbs.

1) I be going to the street fair.

2) They am going with me.

3) I been walking down the road.

4) We has been talking with friends.

5) David am shopping at the store.

6) He be shopping with her.

7) We is riding the bus uptown.

8) Terri been sitting by the window.

9) She am reading today's paper.

10) They has walked to the zoo.

11) You am going to the movie with Al and me.

12) We was working all evening.

13) She am studying for a test.

14) I been looking out the window.

15) They is looking for a place to live.

16) Mary and Tim has been driving all night.

17) Alex and Janet watches videos with Lance.

18) She be in class all day.

19) Joe work at the gas station.

Past tense

The tense of verbs that tells about action in the past.

Verbs that tell about action that was completed in the past are in the **past tense**. There are four past tense verb forms.

EXAMPLES Natalie **played** basketball.
Natalie **was playing** well.
Natalie **had played** many times.
Natalie **had been playing** center.

The helping verbs for past tense are *was, were, had,* and *had been.*

EXAMPLES I **was running**.   You **were running**.
She **had run**.   They **had been running**.

Activity A Number your paper from 1 to 4. Rewrite the following sentence four times. Each time, use a different form of the past tense for the verb *wait*.

Susie, the cat, _____ for a mouse.

Use the correct form of the helping verb *be* in past tense verbs. Remember that a singular subject takes a singular form of the verb. *You* is always considered a plural subject.

EXAMPLES Singular subject: I **was looking**.
He **was watching**.
Plural subject: You **were looking**.
Maria and Tom **were watching**.

- Do not use *done* as a helping verb in past tense verbs.
- The combination *done been* is never correct.
- Use the helping verb *had* with *been* in past tense verbs.

EXAMPLES

Incorrect:	They **done waited** for an hour.
Correct:	They **waited** for an hour.
Correct:	They **were waiting** for an hour.
Incorrect:	They **done been** waiting for a bus.
Correct:	They **had been waiting** for a bus.

Activity B Write these sentences using the correct past tense forms of the verbs.

1) They was heading for home.
2) They had done fished all day.
3) I were fishing, too.
4) We was talking about movies.
5) Jan been walking with her folks.
6) I been waiting for them.
7) We was planting grass in the yard.
8) Mike and Paul was watering the flowers.
9) I done helped them.
10) Frank have bowled a perfect game.
11) Leon been working at the post office.
12) You was waiting at the station.
13) They had done been gone since yesterday.
14) He were watching TV last night.
15) We been waiting for you.
16) He done seen that video three times.
17) The girls was swimming in the pool.
18) I were helping Dwight load the truck.

Future tense

The tense of verbs that tells about action in the future.

Verbs that tell about action that has not yet happened are in the **future tense.** There are four future tense verb forms.

EXAMPLES
Natalie **will play** basketball again.
Natalie **will be playing** hard.
Natalie **will have played** more games.
Natalie **will have been playing** center all season.

All forms of verbs in the future tense need the helping verb *will.* Some future forms need other helping verbs, too. The helping verbs for future tense are *will, will be, will have,* and *will have been.*

EXAMPLES
I **will run.**
She **will have run.**
You **will be running.**
They **will have been running.**

Activity A Number your paper from 1 to 4. Rewrite the following sentence four times. Each time, use a different form of the future tense for the verb *wait.*

Susie, the cat, _____ for a mouse.

• Never use *be* as a helping verb in future tense verbs.
• Always use *will have* with *been* in future tense verbs.

EXAMPLES

Incorrect:	The bus **be** coming soon.
Correct:	The bus **will be** coming soon.
Incorrect:	In a few minutes, they **been waiting** for an hour.
Correct:	In a few minutes, they **will have been waiting** for an hour.

B

U

S

**The bus will be
coming soon.**

Activity B Write these sentences using the correct future tense forms of the verbs. Remember that all verbs in future tense use the helping verb *will*.

1) Brenda and Eddie be doing well.

2) I be doing well next year.

3) Janet sews a new dress tomorrow.

4) The whole group be needing some food.

5) Beth be cooking fish and potatoes.

6) Everyone eating really well.

7) We be working with him.

8) Lots of people be going to that party.

9) Her car be needing new tires soon.

10) Everyone be laughing tonight at the party.

11) Sandra be moving soon.

12) They work hard next year.

13) Jerry sleeps well tonight.

14) The dark clouds drop rain later this afternoon.

15) Stan be taking three tests tomorrow.

16) Marilyn work nights next week.

17) He be sorry tomorrow.

18) Mike be doing better in school next year.

19) I be ready for anything next week.

20) The new play have opened by later this month.

21) We be early for school tomorrow.

22) Susan be moving to Detroit by the end of this project.

23) She be planning a surprise for her friend Gerry.

Negative

A word that means "no" or "not" that stops the action of the verb.

A **negative** is a word that means "no" or "not." Negatives, such as *not* and *never*, often come between the helping verb and the main verb in a verb phrase. Negatives may be used with present, past, and future tense verb forms.

EXAMPLES

Present tense: Sharon **is** *not* **giving** swimming lessons this summer.

Past tense: We **had** *never* **met** our new teacher.

Future tense: She **will** *not* **know** our names.

(The verb phrase in each example sentence is in bold. *Not* and *never* are adverbs. *Not, never*, and shortened words made with *not (n't)* are never part of a verb phrase.)

Activity A Write these sentences on your paper. Underline the verb phrases in the sentences. Circle the negatives.

1) The storm will not be blowing from the east.

2) They will never walk on the beach again.

3) The waves had not covered the whole beach.

4) Waves have not been smashing against the shore for very long.

5) The stores near the beach were not opening their doors.

6) Many people will not forget that awful storm.

7) John has never gone to the beach before, and he has not seen a big storm on the coast.

8) The storm has not arrived yet, but it will not cause much damage.

9) People will not pull their boats from the water.

10) This coast will never be the same.

Activity B Add *not* or *never* to the verbs in these sentences. Write the sentences on your paper. Underline the verb phrases. Then write whether the verb is in *present tense, past tense,* or *future tense.*

Example   The lighthouse had been warning ships of the rocks.

The lighthouse <u>had</u> not <u>been warning</u> ships of the rocks.—past tense

1) Small houses are clustered around the lighthouse.

2) The keeper of the lighthouse is living there.

3) He has been staying in the lighthouse most nights.

4) He will have lived near the lighthouse for seven years.

5) She will hold the meeting here.

6) Others will be coming to her office for the meeting.

7) She will make a deal.

8) She will be building the new place in another six months.

9) Phil and his horse are riding in many events of the rodeo.

10) His horse has jumped over barrels.

11) Phil had roped calves.

12) He had been grabbing wild bulls.

13) Phil had won prizes at the rodeo.

14) Jim has been using his computer every day.

15) He had purchased the latest model.

16) He is playing video games with his friends.

17) This computer will solve all of Jim's problems.

18) It will help him with his homework.

You have learned that regular verbs form their past tense by adding -*d* or -*ed* to their present form. Some regular verbs such as *burn* and *dream* can also add -*t* to form their past tense.

EXAMPLES

Present tense:	burn	dream
Past tense:	burned or burnt	dreamed or dreamt

Irregular verb

A verb that changes its form to form past tenses.

Irregular verbs do not add -*d* or -*ed* to form their past tenses. They form their tenses in other ways. Study this list of irregular verbs. These verbs do not follow any pattern. The only way that you can remember their different forms is to memorize them.

Present	Past	With a Helping Verb
break	broke	(has) broken
bend	bent	(has) bent
burst	burst	(has) burst
catch	caught	(has) caught
come	came	(has) come
drink	drank	(has) drunk
drive	drove	(has) driven
eat	ate	(has) eaten
know	knew	(has) known
ride	rode	(has) ridden
run	ran	(has) run
see	saw	(has) seen
spring	sprang	(has) sprung
swim	swam	(has) swum
take	took	(has) taken
throw	threw	(has) thrown
write	wrote	(has) written

Activity A Write the correct form of each verb in these sentences. Then write whether the verb is *present tense, past tense,* or *future tense.*

1) The three friends have never _____ out to the island. (swim)

2) They _____ some practice laps yesterday. (swim)

3) Sharon will not _____ to the lake with us. (come)

4) The friends have _____ many large fish from that lake. (catch)

5) Over the years, much bait has been _____ into the lake. (throw)

6) The cowboys must have _____ the cattle across the ranch. (drive)

7) They had _____ long and hard for weeks. (ride)

8) At camp, Frank has _____ one calf to the ground. (throw)

9) A cowboy's life has always _____ a lot of hard work. (take)

10) Yesterday, Frank _____ his rope around many cattle. (throw)

11) A pipe in the basement _____ during the night. (burst)

12) The pipe has _____ leaks before. (spring)

13) The water had _____ all over the floor. (run)

14) Next time, we will _____ it in a bucket. (catch)

15) Rita had never _____ anyone as talented as her dance teacher. (know)

16) Rita has _____ of dancing in Broadway shows. (dream)

17) She had _____ her leg badly as a young child (broke).

18) Afterward, she _____ dancing lessons for therapy. (take)

Your writing should create images in the mind of others. A good writer can make readers think they are taking part in the story.

Activity A Write a children's story about a dragon. Have your story take place in the past. Follow the four steps in the writing process.

1. **Prewrite.** Think about stories that children enjoy. Think about dragons and pretend they really did exist sometime in the past.

   > **List words to describe the dragon. Ask:**
   > Is the dragon: friendly? clumsy? brave or not? Does he have a: funny tail? fiery breath? Does he laugh? giggle? or growl?

2. **Write.** Give your dragon a name. Write about what it saw and where it went. Write about what it did. Use your list of describing words.

   > **Example of a beginning:**
   > howard was a silly dragon with a funny tail. he meets a little boy who wanted a ride.

3. **Rewrite.** Look at what you wrote. Would a small child enjoy your story? Is it exciting? Funny? Scary? Can you make it more interesting?

   > **Example of a beginning rewrite:**
   > Once upon a time, a very silly dragon named howard meets a little boy. the boy looks at the big dragon and says in a small brave voice may I have a ride.

4. **Edit.** Check to be sure the verbs are all in the past tense. Check for spelling, end marks, and commas.

> **Example of an edited beginning:**
> Once upon a time, a very silly dragon named Howard met a little boy. The boy looked at the big dragon and said in a small, brave voice, "May I have a ride?"

Activity B Write a story about something that is happening right now. Follow the steps of the writing process.

1. **Prewrite.** Think about a man driving a car, a woman working, or a child playing a game. Choose one of these for the main character in your story.

2. **Write.** Write about what the person is doing now. Where is the person? What's happening? Is the person happy or sad? laughing or crying? running or sitting? eating or sleeping? What will happen to the person by the end of the story?

3. **Rewrite.** Read your story. Is it interesting? Can you improve it? Try to make it better.

4. **Edit.** Look at the verbs you wrote. The story happens in the present time. Are your verbs all in present tense? Check spelling, end marks, and commas.

Activity C Write a story that takes place in the future. Follow the steps of the writing process.

1. **Prewrite.** Think about ways people will travel in the future. Think about spaceships. Pretend a spaceship will take tourists to Jupiter.

2. **Write.** Write about a trip to Jupiter. Who will be on the trip? What funny or scary things will happen on the way?

3. **Rewrite.** Read your story. Is it exciting? Can you make it more interesting? Rewrite sentences to improve your story.

4. **Edit.** Look at the verbs you wrote. Your story takes place in the future. Are your verbs correct? Check spelling, end marks, and commas.

Contraction

A word formed when two words are put together and letters are left out.

A **contraction** is one word made out of two words. A contraction needs an apostrophe. Remember that an apostrophe is a punctuation mark. It takes the place of letters that are left out when the contraction is formed.

EXAMPLES   let + us = let's   **Let's** look at contractions.
that + is = that's   **That's** a good idea.

A pronoun + a helping verb:

I + am = I'm
you + are = you're
we + are = we're
they + are = they're
she, he, it + is = she's, he's, it's

I + will = I'll
you + will = you'll
we + will = we'll
they + will = they'll
she, he, it + will = she'll, he'll, it'll

I + have = I've
you + have = you've
we + have = we've
they + have = they've

I + would = I'd
you + would = you'd
we + would = we'd
they + would = they'd
she, he, it + would = she'd, he'd, it'd

A verb + the adverb *not*:

are + not = aren't
were + not = weren't
has + not = hasn't
is + not = isn't
do + not = don't
does + not = doesn't
did + not = didn't
will + not = won't
could + not = couldn't
would + not = wouldn't
should + not = shouldn't

Find *will* + *not* on the chart on page 174. Notice that the contraction *won't* does not follow the usual pattern for forming contractions. Remember *will* + *not* = *won't*.

Activity A Write the contractions in these sentences correctly on your paper.

1) Its here somewhere.

2) Ive lost it, and its not on the table now.

3) Shell look on that other table for me.

4) It couldnt just walk away.

5) Ill find it soon, and I wont lose it again.

Activity B Change the underlined words in each sentence to a contraction. Write the contractions on your paper.

1) <u>He is</u> having a problem and <u>does not</u> know it.

2) He <u>should not</u> lose things.

3) <u>You are</u> going to keep track of your papers.

4) He <u>did not</u> find that last sheet of paper.

5) He <u>has not</u> looked in the desk, and <u>that is</u> where it is.

Activity C Match the words with their meanings. Write the number and its correct letter on your paper.

Words

1) present

2) past

3) future

4) contraction

5) verb phrase

Meanings

a) yesterday

b) tomorrow

c) helping verb plus main verb

d) today

e) needs an apostrophe

Part A On your paper, write the verb phrase in each sentence.

1) The trip had begun miles away and months ago.

2) Adam has been going through wild country.

3) The wagon has broken down many times.

4) Heat and cold have given him a bad time.

5) He should not have stopped at the creek last night.

Part B Write the correct form of each verb in parentheses.

6) By tonight, Adam will have (rode, ridden) late.

7) He will have (ate, eaten) by the campfire.

8) His mules will have (drank, drunk) from a stream.

9) During the day, Adam will (see, seen) many things from the wagon.

Part C Write the correct present tense form of each verb.

10) Ted (make, makes) phone calls from his desk.

11) By the end of the season, Ted (use, uses) many of his large machines.

12) Each machine (cost, costs) a lot of money.

13) One machine (fill, fills) his tall silo.

14) One machine (feed, feeds) his cattle, while another (weigh, weighs) them.

Part D Number your paper from 15 to 19. Change all the verbs in Part C to past tense. Add helping verbs when needed.

Part E Number your paper from 20 to 24. Change all the verbs in Part C to future tense. Add helping verbs when needed.

Part F Add *not* or *never* to change the meaning of these sentences.

25) Jack has been there.

26) It was fun.

27) Jane likes the place.

28) You will like it.

29) My friends have liked it.

Part G Write these sentences correctly on your paper.

30) sometimes edna cant find the trail

31) she doesnt have a map

32) brutus adams lead mule wont go fast

33) he doesnt have the energy left

34) we dont have a camp for the night

35) the tent wont stay up

36) oh its raining hard now

37) the weather usually warm is turning cold

38) the rubber mattress wont hold air

39) this trip hasnt been much fun

40) brutus the smart mule sleeps under the shade of the trees branches

Test Taking Tip Study any examples that follow a set of directions in a test. Make sure you understand why the example is done as shown. If the example is not clear to you, read the directions again.

Chapter 9

Be Exact

Has this ever happened to you? You and two friends are having a conversation about your favorite television program. You're in the middle of making a terrific point about the star of the show when you notice that one of your friends looks confused. "Exactly *what* are you talking about?" she asks. Suddenly, you all start to laugh. While two of you have been talking about one show, your other friend has been talking about another.

It is important to use exact language when you speak and write. If you know exactly the right words to use, your ideas will be clear and easy to understand.

In this chapter, you will study ways to be more exact when you speak and write.

Goals for Learning

▶ To identify different purposes for personal writing and types of notes

▶ To select accurate verbs in sentences

▶ To use correctly words that sound alike but are spelled differently

▶ To correct sentences with double negatives

▶ To use abbreviations for time of day and year correctly

Have you ever seen an interesting looking person and thought he or she would make a great story character? Have you ever heard a joke and said to yourself, "I should write that down so I don't forget it"? Writing your ideas in a journal is one way to record your thoughts and preserve important memories. You can use any kind of notebook for a journal. Write in it as often as you like.

Activity A Practice writing a journal entry. Use these ideas.

- Put today's date on the top of the page.
- Write about the best part of today.
- Write about the worst part of today.
- Describe something you saw today in as much detail as you can recall. It can be anything—a bird in its nest, a dark rain cloud, a woman selling flowers.

When you want to remember facts and details from class, you can take notes. Notes should include the most important words and ideas. In order to be helpful, reminder notes need to be complete. They also should be neat enough to read and understand.

Activity B On your paper, write reminder notes using only important words from each sentence.

Example   Abraham Lincoln, one of the wisest leaders of this country, was the sixteenth president.
Abraham Lincoln—sixteenth president

1) In 1861, he became president of the United States during a time of trouble between the states.
2) His leadership during the Civil War made Lincoln famous.
3) Lincoln wanted all people to be free.
4) He signed a paper and gave African slaves their freedom.
5) People called him foolish, but he won the war.

Activity C Write the letter of the more complete note in each set. Then use the information in that note to write a more exact sentence.

1) Mary has an appointment.

a)

> dentist

b)

> dentist —
> 8 am,
> Thursday, May 5

2) Paul has an errand to do.

a)

> Buy bread,
> chips, milk.

b)

> Store today.

3) Ann is going downtown.

a)

> Meet a friend in
> front of store this
> afternoon.

b)

> Meet Jane —
> 4 pm
> at 306 Walnut.

The words *accept* and *except* are often confused. *Accept* is a verb that means "to take" or "to receive."

EXAMPLE | Rona will **accept** the call.

Except can be a verb that means "to leave out." It can also be a preposition that means "but."

EXAMPLES

Verb: Coach was happy all season, if you **except** the day of our worst loss.

Preposition: No one was happy **except** the other team.

Activity A On your paper, write the word in parentheses that completes each sentence correctly.

1) The teacher will (except, accept) Sam's answers on the test.

2) He answered all the questions correctly (except, accept) three in the math section.

3) His teacher could not (except, accept) Sam's excuse.

4) All of the students (except, accept) Sam did well in math.

5) Sam will have to (except, accept) a grade of C.

6) He likes school (except, accept) for math.

The verbs *learn* and *teach* are sometimes mixed up. Teach means "to give new facts." *Learn* means "to get new facts."

EXAMPLES | Ann **teaches** math to Walt.

(Ann is giving facts.)

Walt **learns** math from Ann.

(Walt is getting facts.)

Activity B On your paper, write the word in parentheses that completes each sentence correctly.

1) The booklet will (teach, learn) David a skill.
2) David (taught, learned) a skill from the booklet.
3) Mr. Santos (taught, learned) Peter the violin for three years.
4) Someday, Mr. Santos will (teach, learn) his children.
5) Adrian has (taught, learned) violin from Mr. Santos since the age of three.
6) I will (teach, learn) you the state capitals.
7) Lisa will (teach, learn) Ricky some history before the big test.
8) Rosalie (taught, learned) much from the geography instructor.

Activity C On your paper, write the word in parentheses that completes each sentence correctly.

1) Clem (learned, taught) piano to all his sisters (accept, except) the littlest one.
2) Bill will (accept, except) payment from everyone (accept, except) Sara.
3) Those students (learned, taught) every subject from Mr. Adams (accept, except) science.
4) Everyone (accept, except) Tom (learned, taught) something from that last defeat.
5) The bank clerk (accepted, excepted) checks from every student (accept, except) Myra.
6) All those books (learn, teach) math (accept, except) the green one.
7) Rose and Kevin (accept, except) telephone calls from anyone (accept, except) Bert.
8) Henry has (learned, taught) from his sister that everyone earned a B on the test (accept, except) Andy.
9) Anna (learned, taught) me about art and music.
10) I (learned, taught) that they will (accept, except) twenty students into the special math program.

Many people confuse these words: *their, there,* and *they're; your* and *you're; its* and *it's. Their, your,* and *its* are owner pronouns. They do not have apostrophes. *They're, you're,* and *it's* are contractions. Contractions do have apostrophes.

Owner Pronouns	Contractions	Adverb
their	they're = they are	there
your	you're = you are	
its	it's = it is	

There is an adverb that tells where an action takes place.

EXAMPLE   We can walk **there** after school.

Activity A On your paper, write the words in parentheses that complete the sentences correctly.

1) Andy pulled his boat into (their, they're, there) dock.

2) Twin pipes gurgled beneath (its, it's) stern.

3) (Its, It's) a fast one, and (your, you're) lucky.

4) (Their, They're, There) here to see (your, you're) boat.

5) The boat cost more than (their, they're, there) house.

6) (Their, They're, There) go (your, you're) cousin Jessie and her sister.

7) (Their, They're, There) cruising in (their, they're, there) new car.

8) (Their, They're, There) having a great time with (you're, your) friend Emma.

9) (Your, You're) going (their, they're, there) with them later.

10) (Their, They're, There) is homework on (your, you're) desk.

Activity B On your paper, write the words in parentheses that complete the sentences correctly.

1) (Your, You're) puppy is sleeping in (its, it's) new doghouse.

2) (Its, It's) time for the dog's dinner, and (its, it's) dish is gone.

3) (Its, It's) collar is new.

4) (Its, It's) collar sparkles, and (its, it's) leather.

5) After (your, you're) walk, put (its, it's) leash away.

6) (There, They're) goes (your, you're) airplane.

7) (Its, It's) a new Sessnar Skyliner.

8) (Its, It's) cockpit is full of gadgets.

9) Now (its, it's) landing near (its, it's) hangar.

10) (Your, You're) the lucky owner of the plane.

11) (There, They're, Their) sits (your, you're) surprise.

12) (Its, It's) in a big red box.

13) Inside, (there, they're, their) are noisy sounds.

14) People listen. (There, Their, They're) surprised by (its, it's) loud sounds.

15) (Your, You're) careful when you lift (its, it's) lid.

Activity C Find the sentences with mistakes in word usage. Write the sentences correctly on your paper. If a sentence is correct, write C.

1) Rob and Lena put they're books over their on the shelf.

2) The dog is taking it's time with you're newspaper.

3) Wait your turn, please.

4) Your too late for dinner, but its not too late for dessert.

5) The look on there faces was one of shock.

6) I heard your voice, and there you were.

7) You're desk has a scratch on it's right leg.

8) Their not coming to the party at your house.

The verbs *lie* and *lay, sit* and *set,* and *rise* and *raise* are often misused. To avoid confusion with these verbs, first it is important to know the meaning of each word.

Word	Meaning
lie	"to recline" or "to be in a resting position"
lay	"to put" or "to place something"
sit	"to put oneself in a sitting position" (as on a chair)
set	"to place something down"
rise	"to get up" or "to go up"
raise	"to make something go up"

To use these verbs correctly, it is also helpful to know the parts of each verb.

Present	Past	With Helpers
lie	lay	(is) lying, (has) lain
lay	laid	(is) laying, (has) laid
sit	sat	(is) sitting, (has) sat
set	set	(is) setting, (has) set
rise	rose	(is) rising, (has) risen
raise	raised	(is) raising, (has) raised

Finally, it is helpful to know that *lay, set,* and *raise* may each take a direct object. *Lie* and *rise* never take an object. *Sit* almost never takes an object.

EXAMPLES

No direct object: The dog **lay** in front of the fire.

Direct object: The dog **laid** his paw on my lap.

(The dog was in a resting position in front of the fire. The dog placed his paw on the lap. *Paw* is the direct object of *laid*.)

No direct object: Pam **is sitting** on the couch.

Direct object: Ed **set** the book on the table.

(Pam is in an upright position on the couch. Ed put the book on the table. *Book* is the direct object of *set*.)

No direct object: Alice rarely **has risen** before noon.

Direct object: Tina and Leon **have raised** the flag.

(Alice has rarely gotten up before noon. Tina and Leon have made the flag go up. *Flag* is the direct object of *have raised*.)

Activity A Write the verb that completes each sentence correctly. Write the direct object if there is one.

1) The sick child had (lain, laid) in bed for weeks.

2) Her nurse (lay, laid) medicine beside the bed.

3) Her cats are (lying, laying) beside the bed.

4) Books (lay, laid) on the floor all over the room.

5) She will (lie, lay) the papers on the table.

Activity B Write the verb that completes each sentence correctly. Write the direct object if there is one.

1) Enrique had been (sitting, setting) at the head of the table.

2) Together, the men have (sat, set) a plan on paper.

3) The four men (sit, set) around the table and talk.

4) After the meeting, they (sit, set) business aside.

5) They (set, sat) outside, and watched the sun (set, sit).

Activity C Write the verb that completes each sentence correctly. Write the direct object if there is one.

1) The sun will (rise, raise) in another hour.

2) Ed has always (risen, raised) before dawn.

3) He will (rise, raise) the flag at the courthouse.

4) Soon the temperature will (rise, raise) to 100 degrees.

5) His boss will (rise, raise) his hourly pay.

To, too, and *two* are often confused. These words sound alike but mean different things. *To* is a preposition. *Too* is an adverb that means "also" or "too much." *Two* is a number word that can be an adjective or a noun.

EXAMPLES

Preposition:	Ellen and I went **to** the movies.
Adverb:	We were **too** late for the first show.
Adjective:	Luckily, there were **two** shows.
Noun:	The **two** of us enjoyed the movie.

Activity A On your paper, write the word in parentheses that completes each sentence correctly.

1) The stores on Tenth Avenue close (to, too, two) early.

2) Amanda's bike has seats for (to, too, two).

3) Andy's store moved from Fourth Street (to, too, two) Third Avenue.

4) Pete's company moved (to, too, two).

5) My (to, too, two) best friends are Anita and Connie.

6) Tomorrow, we will go (to, too, two) the shore.

The verbs *let* and *leave* are often confused. *Let* means "to allow." *Leave* means "to go away." *Leave* can also mean "to stop" or "to let something stay as it is."

EXAMPLES

Let me into the office. (Allow me into the office.)

Joe **will leave** the office. (Joe will go away from the office.)

Leave the door shut. (Let the door stay in that position.)

Activity B On your paper, write the word in parentheses that completes each sentence correctly.

1) (Leave, Let) Juanita go to the bus station.

2) The bus will (leave, let) early tonight.

3) Katherine didn't (leave, let) the dog out of the house.

4) Both men (leave, let) the office late on Mondays.

5) The small window doesn't (leave, let) the breeze into the study room.

6) (Let, Leave) the dog out now for his walk.

7) Bruce always (lets, leaves) food on his plate.

8) (Let, Leave) me work in peace!

9) (Let, Leave) the window open.

10) You should not (let, leave) anyone disturb you.

Activity C Write the words in parentheses that complete the sentences correctly.

1) (Let, Leave) the light on so I can see (to, too, two).

2) (To, Too, Two) more names have been added (to, too, two) this list.

3) Don't (let, leave) those animals escape from their cages!

4) Anna (let, leave) the airplane engine warm up.

5) (To, Too, Two) many drivers (let, leave) home at seven o'clock.

6) (Let, Leave) Laura go to the hockey game (to, too, two).

7) (Let, Leave) the cat and the monkey come into the house (to, too, two).

8) (Let, Leave) him alone so he can study.

9) Lightning struck Mr. Smith's house (to, too, two) times.

10) (To, Too, Two) many people tried to (let, leave) through the (to, too, two) doors.

You have learned about negatives—words that say *no*. Never use two negatives in the same sentence. A **double negative** is two negatives in one sentence. Double negatives are always incorrect.

Double negative

The mistake of using two words that mean "no" in one sentence.

EXAMPLES

Incorrect: I am not never going there.
Correct: I am not going there.
Correct: I am not ever going there.
Correct: I am never going there.

Here is a list of common negative words. Remember that one negative word in a sentence is enough.

nobody	nothing	nowhere	scarcely
none	no one	no	hardly
not	never		

Not is often used to form contractions. Do not use another negative word in a sentence that has a *not (n't)* contraction.

EXAMPLE

Incorrect: We don't hardly see Phil anymore.
Correct: We don't see Phil much anymore.
Correct: We hardly see Phil anymore.

Here is a list of contractions with *not (n't)*.

aren't	didn't	shouldn't
isn't	don't	can't
wasn't	haven't	won't
weren't	couldn't	hasn't
doesn't	wouldn't	

Activity A Each of these sentences has two or more negative words. Write each sentence correctly on your paper. There may be more than one way to correct each sentence. Write only one correct sentence for each item.

Example   We couldn't see hardly nothing in the dark alley.

We couldn't see anything in the dark alley.

We could see nothing in the dark alley.

We could hardly see anything in the dark alley.

1) Carlos and Sheila didn't see nobody on the street.

2) They didn't see nobody come out of the burning house.

3) Nobody saw nothing strange during the fire.

4) They will not never go near that house again.

5) The old car cannot go no more down the road.

6) It don't have no power for hills.

7) The brakes don't work no more.

8) She will not buy no more old cars.

9) Mr. Burton won't never live in an old apartment again.

10) His heater doesn't give no heat.

11) His neighbor never gives him no peace.

12) He didn't get no sleep during the last two nights.

13) The windows don't hardly open.

14) The doors aren't scarcely any better.

15) The sofa doesn't have no springs.

16) The owner can't afford no repairs.

17) The owner won't tell Mr. Burton nothing.

18) Mr. Burton won't pay no more money out of his pocket for rent.

Writers use contrasting words and ideas to help readers understand the differences between two or more things or ideas. For example, you might enjoy one school activity but dislike another. You could contrast the favorable points of the activity you like to the negative points of the activity you dislike. On the other hand, you might enjoy both activities but for different reasons. Then you would contrast the reasons each activity appeals to you.

The following is a review of the four steps of the writing process. The example is a contrast between two sports—baseball and football.

1. **Prewrite.** The first thing you do before writing is decide what you want to write about. Gather your thoughts and arrange them so that your ideas will be easily understood.

baseball?	football?
slow pace	fast action
easy to follow	

2. **Write.** Put your thoughts on paper. Write as quickly as you can. Don't worry about mistakes. Just write the ideas. You can correct mistakes later.

   > Which do I like to watch the best? Football or baseball? Baseball is slow Football has lots of action. I like both. One is easy to follow. I like both sports.

3. **Rewrite.** You want your writing to express your meaning. Go back and read what you wrote. How can it be improved? Rewrite those sentences that are unclear.

   > I like both football and baseball, Its hard for me to decide which one I like best Footbal has more action but baseball is easiest to follow

4. Edit. Now read your work and correct any mistakes you find. Be sure to check for correct spelling and clear sentences.

> I like both football and baseball. It's hard to decide which one I like better. Football has more action, but baseball is easier to follow.

Writing

Practice

Writing Practice

Activity A Use the writing process to compare cars. Think about two kinds of cars. Which car do you like better? Why do you like it better? Rewrite and edit your comparison to make it better and easier to understand.

Activity B Use the writing process to write a paragraph about where you would like to live—a farm, a city, or a small town. Which place would make you the happiest? Why is that place best for you? Describe the features of the place that make it better than the others. Write ideas as they come to you. Then rewrite and edit your paragraph.

Activity C Use the writing process to write a paragraph about the kind of movies you like. Think about comedies, action movies, horror movies, or science fiction. Which do you enjoy most? Why do you think that type of movie is the best? Write ideas as you think of them. Then rewrite and edit.

Activity D Use the writing process to describe an actor on television or in the movies. Think about the person and the kinds of things he or she says and does. What does the actor do that you like? Why? What does the actor do that you don't like? Do your friends like the same actor? Why, or why not? Write ideas as quickly as they come to you. Then rewrite and edit.

You can write about time in several ways. Days of the week and months of the year are capitalized. However, seasons are not capitalized. Also, the days of the week and some months of the year have **abbreviations**. An abbreviation is a short form of a word. Abbreviations for the days and the months should never be used when writing sentences.

Abbreviation

Short form of a word.

One way to write the time of day is with a **colon** (:). A colon is a punctuation mark that separates the hour from the minutes in time.

Colon (:)

A punctuation mark used in time.

EXAMPLES

Time:	It's 6:00 A.M. It's 6 o'clock. It's six o'clock.
Days:	Monday, Friday, Sunday
Dates and Special Days:	March 17 is St. Patrick's Day.
Seasons:	spring, summer, autumn, winter
Date:	Friday, July 4, 1997

Activity A On your paper, write these sentences correctly. Put in the missing punctuation marks and capital letters.

1) his flight left on saturday at 730 AM

2) it arrived in texas at 403 PM

3) the last flight left at 4 oclock

4) james made the trip last summer on july 15

5) the 1005 AM train is running late

6) the red-eye flight leaves at 1115 PM on thursday june 24 1999

Activity B Write the full word for each abbreviation.

1) Sun.   **5)** Thurs

2) Mon.   **6)** Fri.

3) Tues.   **7)** Sat.

4) Wed.   **8)** Jan.

9) Feb.   **13)** Sept.

10) Mar.   **14)** Oct.

11) Apr.   **15)** Nov.

12) Aug.   **16)** Dec.

Activity C Write each sentence correctly. Change abbreviations to the complete word. Add missing punctuation marks and capital letters.

1) joe set his alarm for 8 oclock on june 1 2001

2) it rang on time every mon through fri that summer

3) on nov 12 his clock stopped at 437 AM

4) every fall squirrels gather nuts in oct and nov from the tree outside joes window

5) the noisy animals woke joe at 5 AM one mon

6) aug 8 1935 was on a thur

7) my parents flight from rome arrived promptly at 630 PM

8) the theater opens the first fri in oct

9) it closes after the winter season on the last tue in mar

10) tony made a phone call last wed at 1130 AM

11) summer school ended on july 30 1999

12) in that state farmers plant crops in late mar and harvest them in early oct

13) joan closed the cottage for the winter at noon on sept 15

14) next wed the 1115 AM flight to detroit will leave at 2 oclock

15) drama students perform their fall play in nov and their spring play in apr

Part A On your paper, write the word in parentheses that completes each sentence correctly.

1) Adam will (accept, except) a job at the laundry.

2) There weren't (no, any) other jobs.

3) (Too, To, Two) many people wanted (too, to, two) work at the laundry.

4) Adam stayed (there, their, they're) until he got the job.

5) (It's, Its) hours are tough, and (it's, its) true that the owners do not pay well; however, (their, they're, there) nice to (their, they're, there) workers.

6) Adam will go (they're, their, there) early in the morning.

7) (Your, You're) going (there, they're, their) with him; don't forget (your, you're) lunch.

Part B Write the following sentences correctly.

8) the man on the street never saw no pot of flowers

9) our bus stops here at 445 PM every day but sat

10) I haven't never seen nothing like it

11) tom went to the cabin on the last sun in dec

12) nobody didn't never mean to hurt him

13) cara finishes work in the summer at 5 oclock

Part C Write notes using important words from each sentence.

14) On Monday, March 24th, Frank has an appointment with the dentist at 10 A.M.

15) When Anna goes to the grocery store, she needs to buy canned peas, bread, dog food, and a large package of napkins. At the pet store, she needs to buy hamster food.

16) Raymond has basketball practice at 8 A.M. on Saturday, January 7, in the school's gym. The back door will be unlocked.

17) LaToya was elected class president on September 13th. The student council counted the votes.

18) Marty will leave on Red Ball Airlines on April 23. He will be on Flight 743, leaving from Springfield Airport at 2:10 P.M.

Part D Write each sentence correctly.

19) eva (lay, laid) in the sun until 430 PM

20) after you (sit, set) the table, (sit, set) down near the window

21) a poor test score last sept (learned, taught) fred a lesson about homework

22) before 1000 AM the temperature inside the house will (rise, raise) 25 degrees

23) (your, you're) remote control box (lies, lays) under the sofa

24) last wed the mail carrier had (laid, lain) three small boxes at the door

25) smoke (rose, raised) from a pan of beans (setting, sitting) on the stove

Test Taking Tip Do you have to take a matching test? First, match all the items that you know. Cross them out. Then try to match the items that are left.

Chapter

10

Making Sentences Work

How do you get to know the characters in a story? One way is by paying attention to what the characters say. You can learn a lot about people in a story by what they say and how they say it. In life, people express their ideas and feelings through the words they speak. The sound of a person's voice also provides clues to how the person feels. When you read a story, you cannot "hear" the sound of a character's voice. So writers have to help you imagine what a character sounds like. Writers do this through word choice, punctuation, and a variety of sentence structures.

In this chapter, you will study how to communicate people's spoken words and feelings in your writing.

Goals for Learning

▶ To use punctuation to show feelings
▶ To write various types of sentences
▶ To analyze sentence parts in questions
▶ To identify complex and compound-complex sentences
▶ To punctuate spoken words correctly

Tone of voice
The sound of speech.

A speaker's words send one message. The **tone of voice,** or sound of the speaker's voice, can reinforce the message or change its meaning. One way to communicate a speaker's tone of voice in writing is through end punctuation.

A sentence that ends in a period makes a statement. The speaker's tone of voice is quiet or neutral. The speaker's message is communicated mainly through the meaning of the words.

A sentence that ends in an exclamation point shows excitement or strong feeling. The speaker's tone of voice expresses extreme joy, sorrow, horror, surprise, or another strong feeling. An exclamation point tells readers to pay attention. The speaker is saying something that is important to him or her.

A sentence that ends in a question mark asks a question. The speaker's tone of voice is curious. It asks *Why? What? How? When?* or *Who?* A question mark makes the reader wonder, "What next?"

Notice how different end punctuation changes the meaning and tone of voice of the following sentence.

EXAMPLES

Mia came in first in the talent contest.

(The period shows that the speaker's tone of voice is neutral. The speaker is stating a fact without expressing any particular feeling.)

Mia came in first in the talent contest!

(The exclamation point shows that the speaker's tone of voice is expressing strong feeling, such as happiness or surprise.)

Mia came in first in the talent contest?

(The question mark shows that the speaker's tone of voice is expressing curiosity, perhaps even disbelief.)

Activity A On your paper, rewrite each of the following sentences. Add end punctuation marks that express different tones of voice.

1) What a day this is

2) I've told you about this before

3) I won't be going to camp this year

4) Thank you for the beautiful gift

5) What is going on here

Interjections can also be used to express tone of voice. Interjections that are followed by a comma express mild feelings. Interjections that are followed by an exclamation point show strong feelings.

> **EXAMPLES**   Well, look at the time.
>
> (The comma after the interjection shows that the speaker is mildly concerned about the time.)
>
>   Well! Look at the time!
>
> (The exclamation points show that the speaker is excited or upset about the time.)

Activity B Rewrite these sentences. Choose punctuation marks that show the tone of voice. Use capital letters after interjections punctuated with an exclamation point.

1) What we have a test today

2) Well I didn't know about it

3) Okay I'll do the best I can

4) Look a new movie is in town

5) Hey it has the biggest stars

6) Yes the papers say it's great

7) Oh my friend Bob saw that movie three times

8) Well let's see it on Saturday

Activity C Write a short story about an exciting event. Remember to use punctuation that shows tone of voice.

A sentence can make a statement, ask a question, give a command, or make a request.

EXAMPLES

Statement:	I can help you.
Question:	May I help you?
Command or request:	Help me, please.
Strong command or request:	Help me, now!

Activity A Follow the directions and write your own sentences. Use the examples above to help you.

1) Write a statement using the word *save*.

2) Write a question using the word *save*.

3) Write a command using the word *save*.

4) Write a strong request using the word *save*.

5) Write a statement using the word *stop*.

6) Write a question using the word *stop*.

7) Write a command using the word *stop*.

8) Write a strong request using the word *stop*.

The words *can* and *may* are often used in place of each other, but they have different meanings. To use *can* and *may* correctly, remember these rules:

• Use *can* to show someone is able to do something.

• Use *may* to show that someone is allowed to do something or to show the possibility that something will happen.

EXAMPLES

Tara **can** sing now.
(Tara is able to sing now.)

Tara **may** sing now.
(Tara has permission to sing now,
or maybe Tara will sing now.)

Activity B Use *can* or *may* to write a sentence for each of these ideas.

I am able to:	Maybe I will:
swim	go to a movie
play ball	do my homework
study	cut my hair
sleep	sleep
eat lunch	eat lunch

Activity C Write one question, one statement, one request, and one strong request for each group of words below.

1) John has money problems.

2) Paula was offered a job.

3) What a difference a day makes.

4) The computer is broken.

5) Susan left for Detroit today.

6) William won a prize on a game show.

Activity D Write the letter of the correct meaning of each sentence.

a)	The person is giving a strong command.
b)	The person is able.
c)	The person is giving or asking permission.
d)	The person is making a mild request.

1) She may work at the store.

2) He can work at the store.

3) Get to work now!

4) May I work at the store?

5) I can go to the dance with you.

6) May I go to the dance with you?

7) You may dance with me.

8) Dance with me now!

A sentence that asks a question ends with a question mark. Some questions begin with pronouns. A pronoun used to form a question is called a **question pronoun**. The pronouns *who, whom, whose, what,* and *which* are question pronouns.

Question pronoun

A pronoun that asks.

> **EXAMPLES**   **Who** knocked on the door?
> **Whose** is this?

Other words that are used to form questions include the adverbs *when, where, why,* and *how* and helping verbs such as *will, can, do, have, could, should,* and *would.*

> **EXAMPLES**   **When** will they arrive?
> **Did** you see that?

When the pronoun *who* begins a question with an action verb, *who* is usually the subject of the sentence. Other question pronouns may also be the subject of action verbs, or they may describe the subject.

> **EXAMPLES**   **Who** knocked on the door?
> **What** made that smell?
> **Which** of these keys opens the lock?
> **Whose** book fell on the floor?

In questions with linking verbs, the subject often follows the verb. The subject of a question may also come between the helping verb and the main verb. Keep in mind that *whom* is an objective case pronoun and can never be the subject of a sentence.

> **EXAMPLES**   What is your **name**?
> Whom did **Mom** see at the lake?
> Why were **you** so late?
> Are **Nick** and **Mike** at home?

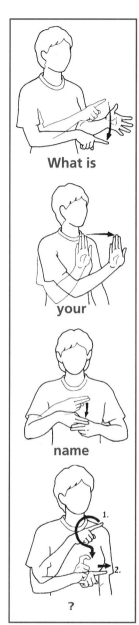

What is

your

name

?

What is your name?

To find the subject in a question, follow the steps in this example:

EXAMPLE | **What did the children eat for dinner?**
- Find the verb or verb phrase. **did eat**
- Ask *Who*? or *What*? about the verb. **Who did eat?**
- Try to form a statement from the question. **The children did eat what for dinner.**
- Identify the subject. **children**

Activity A Write each question on your paper. Use the above steps to find the subject and verb of each question. Underline the subject. Circle the verb or verb phrase.

1) Did your friends sit near you?

2) Will that stack of books help you with the test?

3) Has Evan parked his car by the pool?

4) Could you bring that book over here?

5) Who runs the old store in town?

6) When does the corner store open?

7) Which of the barrels is on sale?

8) Who bought all that candy?

9) What will Ilana and Michael find upstairs?

10) Is your class a good one?

11) Are the students in your class friendly?

12) Where are my keys?

Activity B Use these words to form questions. Write each question on your paper and underline its subject.

1) who

2) what

3) whose

4) which

5) when

6) where

7) why

8) how

9) will

10) did

11) can

12) are

You learned in Chapter 3 that a compound sentence has two complete thoughts joined by a conjunction or by a semicolon. Conjunctions such as *and, but,* and *or* join main ideas in a compound sentence.

EXAMPLES

Compound sentence: Al loves dogs, but his sister is allergic to dog hair.

complete thought   complete thought

Complex sentence

A sentence that includes both an independent clause and a dependent clause.

A **complex sentence** has an **independent clause** and a **dependent clause.** An independent clause expresses a complete thought and is a sentence. A dependent clause does not express a complete thought. It is not a sentence and cannot stand alone.

Independent clause

A complete sentence.

EXAMPLES

Complex sentence:	Al works at a dog kennel after school because he loves dogs.
Independent clause:	Al works at a dog kennel after school (a complete thought)
Dependent clause:	because he loves dogs (not a complete thought)

Dependent clause

A group of words that does not form a complete thought and cannot stand alone.

Dependent clauses are joined to independent clauses by dependent clause conjunctions.

Dependent Clause Conjunctions			
after	before	so that	whenever
although	if	unless	where
as	once	until	wherever
because	since	when	while

Activity A Write each complex sentence on your paper. Underline the independent clause once and the dependent clause twice. Circle the conjunction.

Example Ben's car doesn't work well (since) it is so old.

1) He watches for engine overheating if the hill is steep.

2) His car struggles up the hill while traffic waits.

3) An old car can't climb a steep hill unless it's in good shape.

4) He is surprised whenever his car starts.

5) I want ice water when I'm really thirsty.

6) Tom wants a steak, although he's not very hungry.

7) Jenny wants a new coat since the old one is too small.

8) Fred wants a new bike while he is in middle school.

Compound-complex sentence

A sentence with two or more independent clauses and one or more dependent clauses.

A sentence can be both compound and complex. A **compound-complex sentence** has two or more independent clauses and at least one dependent clause.

EXAMPLES

Compound-complex
sentence: Al likes big, noisy dogs, and I like pets that are quiet.

                     two independent clauses   dependent clause

Activity B Write whether a sentence is *compound, complex,* or *compound-complex.*

1) Carla's grocery cart was full; she shopped for the month.

2) The clerk rang up Carla's order, which filled twenty bags.

3) We got out of the car, and the dog, which had been asleep on the front porch, sat up and barked.

4) The dog is friendly, but since his bark is so loud, he can seem scary to strangers.

5) Carla and I talked while we prepared a dinner of baked stuffed shrimp, green beans, and salad.

6) Because Carla bought so much food, the cabinets were full and her whole family was happy.

In some complex sentences, pronouns relate or tie a dependent clause to the rest of the sentence. The pronoun is the subject of the clause.

Pronouns That Begin Dependent Clauses
that   what   whatever   which   who

EXAMPLE

Amy, **who goes to my school**, almost won the spelling contest.

A dependent clause can appear at the beginning, in the middle, or at the end of a complex sentence. Use a comma when the dependent clause comes at the beginning or in the middle of the sentence. Do not use a comma when the dependent clause comes at the end of the sentence.

EXAMPLES

Because they were hungry, Noah and Lee went out for pizza.

Noah and Lee, **who were hungry,** went out for pizza.

Noah and Lee went out for pizza **because they were hungry**.

Activity A On your paper, write each sentence. Underline the dependent clause. Add commas where needed.

1) Unless his brother goes with him Matthew won't go out.

2) Napoli's pizza place which has the best pizza in town is their favorite restaurant.

3) Matthew who loves video games plays and eats at the same time.

4) They stay at Napoli's until their friends arrive.

5) Because it has the best pizza the friends always meet at Napoli's.

Some conjunctions that introduce dependent clauses are also prepositions or part of two-word prepositions. These include *after, before, since, until, as of,* and *because of.*

Do not confuse a prepositional phrase with a dependent clause. A dependent clause has a subject and a verb. A prepositional phrase does not.

Dependent clause:	We met for pizza **after the show ended**.
Prepositional phrase:	We met for pizza **after the show**.

Activity B Write whether the underlined words in each sentence are a *dependent clause* or a *prepositional phrase*.

1) <u>Before the game</u>, Jon and Sheri studied.

2) <u>Before the game began</u>, Jon and Sheri studied at the library.

3) <u>After the game ended</u>, Jon and Sheri went to the park.

4) <u>After the game</u>, Lamont and Dave went to the pool.

Complex sentences combine related ideas. Writers use complex sentences to add interest and variety.

Related ideas:	The Olympics are over.
	The spirit remains.
Complex sentence:	Although the Olympics are over, the spirit remains.

Activity C Combine each pair of sentences to make a complex sentence. Use the conjunction in parentheses. Write the sentences on your paper.

1) Athletes can't win. They practice often. (unless)

2) They trained hard. They felt ready. (until)

3) The athletes are heroes. They go around the world. (wherever)

4) Math is an important subject. It is hard for some students. (which)

5) John studies his lessons at night. He earns good grades. (who)

Direct quotation

The exact words that someone says.

Quotation marks (" ")

Punctuation used to begin and end a direct quotation.

Indirect quotation

What someone says but not his or her exact words.

A **direct quotation** is the exact words that someone says. Use **quotation marks (" ")** to enclose the words of a direct quotation. An **indirect quotation** uses other words to tell what someone says. Do not use quotation marks with an indirect quotation.

EXAMPLES

Direct quotation: Ray said, **"That was a great movie!"**

Indirect quotation: Ray told Phil **that the movie was great.**

Activity A On your paper, write whether the underlined words in each sentence are a *direct quotation* or *indirect quotation*.

1) Phil said, <u>"Let's go see a movie."</u>

2) Ray said <u>that he would ask Erica to go.</u>

3) Erica said <u>that she was dying to see that movie.</u>

4) <u>"If you pay for the movie, I'll pay for the popcorn,"</u> she said.

5) Phil said, <u>"That's a great idea."</u>

6) During the movie, Erica said <u>that the ending was sad.</u>

7) <u>"I don't want to know!"</u> Ray said.

Follow these rules when writing sentences with direct quotations:

- Capitalize the first word of a direct quotation that is a complete sentence. Always capitalize the first word of a direct quotation that begins a sentence, even if it is not a complete sentence.

- Place a comma right after the words that identify the speaker when the speaker's name comes before the quotation. Place the comma before the final quotation mark when the speaker's name follows the quotation.

- Place the period before the final quotation mark when the quotation ends a sentence that is a statement.

> Erica said, **"Sad movies make me cry."**
> **"Everything makes you cry,"** Phil joked.

Activity B Rewrite the following indirect quotations as direct quotations.

1) Kim said that Candace knows a good play we should see.

2) Candace said that the play will run another month.

3) Andy and Sheila said that they were going to visit next month.

4) They said that they would like to see the play, too.

5) Candace said that she would like to see the play again.

6) Candace said that she would take Andy and Sheila with her.

A direct quotation can be more than one sentence long. Use only one set of quotation marks to enclose the speaker's entire speech.

> Erica said, **"The popcorn was good. Now I want some ice cream."**

Activity C Rewrite the following indirect quotations as direct quotations.

1) Mary said that she is tired of movies. She prefers TV shows.

2) Alice said that she prefers movies. She likes an evening at the theater.

3) Mary said that it is easier to change channels. She said that she can watch a couple of shows at the same time.

4) Alice said that she can't do that. She said that she gets confused.

5) Mary said that Alice should come and spend an evening with her. Mary said that she would show Alice her method of watching two TV shows.

It is important to edit your writing carefully. Here are some helpful hints for proofreading your work.

- Look for mistakes in grammar, punctuation, and spelling.
- Check to see that every sentence has a subject and verb and that it expresses a complete thought.
- Make sure every sentence begins with a capital letter and ends with a punctuation mark.
- Check that the subject and the verb agree. (Singular subjects takes singular verbs. Plural subjects take plural verbs.)
- Make sure that you use the correct form of a verb to tell about past, present, and future time.

Activity A On your paper, answer each of the following questions.

1) What are the parts of the writing process?

2) What are the two main parts of a sentence?

3) What are three punctuation marks that end sentences?

4) What are the eight parts of speech?

Activity B Find and edit the mistakes in each sentence.

1) jake called come and eat dinner

2) everyone were hungry no one had ate since breakfast

3) she work hard on the ranch for the past week

4) after people works hard their hungry

5) jake a good cook grills thick steaks

6) helen told us that she took a trip to her uncles ranch in texas

7) uncle ted and helen talked abot there horses while jake grilled steaks potatoes and fresh corn

8) at last we can eat someone yelled

9) your a great cook i said to jake

When you write, try to include a variety of sentence types. Remember that you can combine ideas in compound, complex, or compound-complex sentences.

EXAMPLES

Simple: The sun rose. The sun set. The day ended.
Compound: The sun rose, and then it set; the day ended.
Complex: The sun set as the day ended.
Compound-Complex: The sun rose and, as the day ended, the sun set.

Activity C Combine the ideas in these simple sentences into compound, complex, or compound-complex sentences. Write at least one sentence of each type.

1) The dog barked. The cat scratched. They fought.

2) The ball bounced. The player jumped. The game ended.

3) Lights dimmed. Music played. The movie started.

4) Monkeys screech. Lions roar. The zoo opens.

5) A rooster crows. A robin sings. A new day dawns.

Activity D Use the steps in the writing process to write a story about Caroline. Use a variety of sentence types and quotations in your story. Use this information.

Emma asked Caroline to a party. Caroline said she would go. She doesn't know many of the people who will be at that party. Later, her best friend asks her to another party. She talks to her friends about the problem.

1) What do Caroline's friends say? What does Caroline decide to do? What does she tell Emma and her best friend?

2) Rewrite and edit your short story about Caroline.

A direct quotation may stand alone.

EXAMPLE

"A penny saved is a penny earned."

The name of the person who is being quoted can come before, after, or in the middle of the quotation. Notice the placement of the commas that separate the speaker from the quotation in each of these examples.

EXAMPLES

Benjamin Franklin said, "A penny saved is a penny earned."
"A penny saved," said Benjamin Franklin, "is a penny earned."
"A penny saved is a penny earned," said Benjamin Franklin.

If a quotation is a question or an exclamation, place the question mark or exclamation point before the final quotation mark.

EXAMPLES

"Where have you been?" Kerry asked.
Susan exclaimed, **"What an exciting city Detroit is!"**
(Notice that no comma is needed before Kerry's name. No end punctuation is usually needed after the quotation marks that enclose an exclamation or a question that ends a sentence.)

Activity A Write these sentences correctly on your paper.

1) Paula said welcome to my cafe

2) Where is the meat I ordered asked Louie

3) What great shrimp this is Bill exclaimed

4) It's my secret family recipe said Louie

5) Tom asked quietly justin are you asleep

6) justin's father yelled I thought you were working on the lawn

7) I was working said justin but I took a break

Repeating the verb *said* in sentences can make your writing sound dull. Here is a list of other verbs you can use in place of *said* when writing direct quotations.

yell	whisper	declare
laugh	call out	ask
exclaim	mumble	gasp

Activity B Stan is at a ball game. Write Stan's comments as direct quotations. Try not to repeat the word *said* in your sentences. Look at the list above for words you can use in place of *said*.

Example: Let's play ball
Stan yelled, "Let's play ball!"

1) when will this game begin

2) I hope it doesn't rain

3) that was a nice catch

4) don't stop run for third base

5) send in a new pitcher

6) why don't you use your fast ball

7) watch that runner at second base

8) what a great game this is

Activity C Write these compound and complex sentences. Add capital letters and punctuation.

1) the day was a long one and now i am very tired

2) new york is a nice city but i prefer detroit

3) january is cold june is warm

4) as i sit here i think about my friends and my family

5) joe left when the music stopped

6) when class began mary wasn't here

7) apples are good grapes are great but my favorite are plums

8) denver salt lake city and dallas are great cities but they're not detroit

Part A Match the words with their meanings. Write the number and its correct letter on your paper.

Words	Meanings
1) complex sentence	a) exact words of speaker
2) question	b) has a dependent clause
3) indirect quotation	c) has two complete thoughts
4) compound sentence	d) asks
5) direct quotation	e) does not use exact words of speaker

Part B On your paper, write the subject and the complete verb for each question.

6) Why does Sam still use that old computer?

7) Has he written good stories on it?

8) Does it work well?

9) Where did Sam buy it?

10) When will Sam sell it?

11) Which bike at the curb belongs to David?

12) Is the wind rattling the chain on the door?

13) Will the ice on the lake crush the boat against the dock?

Part C Make four columns on your paper. Label them *Subject, Verb, Question Pronoun,* and *Adverb*. Write the subject, verb, and question pronoun or adverb in each of these questions.

14) Why is the cat fat?

15) Which of the books did you write?

16) When will the next bus stop at this corner?

17) Where are Jake and Rick going?

18) Who are the new students in class?

19) How did you learn about the contest?

20) What has Lisa done with the car keys?

Part D Write these sentences correctly on your paper. Use punctuation and capital letters.

21) where does the dirt road lead bill asked

22) mrs smith asked what are you doing

23) alice yelled the last movie begins in two minutes

24) i can't do it josie sighed

25) you can if you try lena exclaimed

Part E Write these sentences on your paper. Underline the independent clause once and the dependent clause twice.

26) The team that won the World Series was from Atlanta.

27) Mr. Andrews, who knows about baseball, will speak at the meeting.

28) Whatever happens, the play will open Saturday.

29) The Dodge Viper, which has 400 horsepower, left every other car on the track behind.

30) She is someone whose word you can trust.

Part F Write whether each sentence is *compound, complex,* or *compound-complex.*

31) When the class bell rang, some students were in the hall.

32) Because the day was hot, Earl went home early, and Jana went swimming.

33) I will go to the beach unless it rains.

34) Mountains are high; valleys are low; the plains are flat.

35) Andy ran toward the monkey cage after the zoo opened.

Test Taking Tip

When taking a true-false test, read each statement carefully. Write true only when the statement is totally true. Write false if part or all of the statement is false.

11

Writing for Others

Do you enjoy writing letters? You write letters mainly to communicate with others. How do you make your letters interesting and fun for the people who read them? Do you share important details of your life and the lives of those close to you? Do you include humorous stories about yourself?

A letter is one form of written communication. There are other forms, such as memos, invitations, news articles, directions, stories, and reviews. Whenever you write, your goal is to share information and ideas with readers. To be sure readers understand your ideas, you must present them in a clear, organized way.

In this chapter, you will study different forms of written communication.

Goals for Learning

▶ To write facts in memos, invitations, and news stories
▶ To write paragraphs that describe, that give directions, and that persuade
▶ To write a story, a review, and a letter

Imagine this scene: The phone rings. You answer it. It's for your friend who is out. You take a message, making sure that you write the information clearly and accurately.

People in offices handle situations like this every day. An important part of their jobs is their ability to take and give messages clearly and accurately.

Memo

A clear, organized record of important facts and details.

Many office workers record important messages in **memos.** A memo records facts and details in a clear, organized way. The person reading the memo should not have any questions about the message or its purpose. Look at the example memo below.

EXAMPLE On September 15 at 1:00 P.M., Nick called. Bill answered the phone. Nick told Bill that it was very important that Carlo call him back that day before 6:00 P.M. at 945-2216.

MEMO

To: Carlo

From: Bill

Subject: Phone call from Nick

Date: Sept. 15

Time: 1:00 P.M.

He says it is important that you call him back before 6 P.M. today at 945-2216.

Activity A On your paper, write a memo for each of these phone calls. Use the example as your model.

1) Linda called for Joey on December 1 at 3:30 P.M. She wants him to meet her at the corner of 5th and Elm Streets at 5 P.M.

2) Peter called for Aaron on January 7 at 7 P.M. He wants to borrow one of Aaron's cassette tapes.

3) Kim called on April 2 at 8 P.M. She wants Karen to call her tomorrow at work. The number is 766-7011.

Invitation

A written request.

An **invitation** is a written request. An invitation asks someone to attend a party, a meeting, a lunch, or other event. Like a memo, an invitation presents important information in a clear, organized way. Invitations tell:

- what the event is and, usually, its purpose
- when, where, and at what time the event will take place
- who is arranging the event

Most invitations also include a telephone number for an RSVP. This means "please reply" to tell whether you can or cannot attend the event. Often, a date by which to reply is also given. This helps the person planning the event know how many people will be attending. Here is an example of a party invitation.

You're invited to a party!

When:	December 3
What Time:	7 P.M.
Where:	1340 Weatherworn Way, Apt. C, Blairsville, California
Given by:	Faith Redmond
	To celebrate Josh Redmond's 16th birthday
RSVP:	738-2072, by November 15

Activity B Write an invitation to each of these parties.

1) Everett Hull is having a New Year's Eve party on December 31 at 9:00 P.M. at 16 Holland Street, New Haven, Wisconsin. He would like guests to reply by December 20. His phone number is 223-7102.

2) Katie Thomas is having a graduation party on June 2 at 2 P.M. at 201 South Fourth Street, Brighton, Arkansas. Her phone number is 678-4003.

3) Bill McKay and Jill Johnson are getting engaged. Jill's younger sister Amy is having a party for them at 7 P.M. on March 4 at 601 West Main in Waterloo, Iowa. Amy's phone number is 811-1767. She wants guests to reply by February 15.

News stories give us facts about current events. We hear news reports on radio and television. We read news articles in newspapers and magazines. The **lead paragraph** in a news article answers the questions *Who? What? Where? When? Why?* and sometimes, *How?*

Lead paragraph

A paragraph that introduces a news article; it tells who, what, when, where, why, and sometimes, how.

EXAMPLE

Local Woman Wins Prize

Maria Woods, 1206 Pine Road, won first prize at the county fair last Saturday for her giant carrots. The carrots raised by Woods were over three pounds each. When asked how she grew such big carrots, Woods replied, "Good, rich soil and my granddad's secret fertilizer mix."

Who:	Maria Woods
What:	won first prize
Where:	at the county fair
When:	last Saturday
Why:	for her carrots
How:	rich soil and granddad's secret fertilizer mix

Activity A Read this lead paragraph for a news article. Find the facts that answer the questions below. Write the facts on your paper.

Griggs Wins Sports Award

Scott Griggs, 409 East Plaza Blvd., was named "Most Valuable Player of the Year" by the Sloane Chamber of Commerce at a picnic last Friday. Griggs' forkball helped him pitch five no-hitters for the Sloane Sweat Sox last season. The team finished in first place.

1) Who?

2) What?

3) Where?

4) When?

5) Why?

6) How?

Activity B Use the steps of the writing process to write a lead paragraph for a news article about each of the events outlined below.

1. **Prewrite** The facts are given for you to use.

2. **Write** Turn the facts into sentences. Write quickly. Do not worry about mistakes in spelling and grammar. You can correct them later.

3. **Rewrite** Improve your sentences. Look at the example news story for help.

4. **Edit** Read your work and correct all mistakes.

   1) *Who:* Joshua Hirsch
      What: arrived from Israel
      When: Tuesday
      Where: New York City
      Why: to see a brother he hasn't seen in fifty years

   2) *Who:* Joe Santos
      What: won Dry Gulch Auto Race
      When: Saturday
      Where: Reno, Nevada
      Why: best time for the track
      How: fastest car and best pit crew

   3) *Who:* Wanda Harper
      What: slept on her roof
      When: Thursday night
      Why: to escape floodwaters when dam broke
      How: "I climbed out attic window and onto the roof."

   4) *Who:* Ella Schmidt
      What: won music contest
      When: Friday
      Where: Park College
      Why: played guitar and drums
      How: played original songs with well-known favorites

   5) *Who:* Gus Wilson
      What: caught a catfish weighing 20 pounds
      When: Thursday evening
      Where: Black Lagoon, Memphis
      Why: to win contest for biggest fish
      How: used old-fashioned bait—ordinary earthworms

Descriptive paragraph
A paragraph that describes a person, place, or thing.

Paragraph
A group of sentences about one topic.

Topic
The main idea of an essay or paragraph.

Topic sentence
A sentence that states the main idea of a paragraph.

A **paragraph** is a group of sentences that tells about one **topic,** or main idea. The **topic sentence** states the main idea of the paragraph. The other sentences in the paragraph relate to, or support, the main idea.

A descriptive paragraph describes a person, place, or thing. Use the steps of the writing process to write a descriptive paragraph.

1. **Prewrite** Think about a topic. Jot it down. List facts about your topic, along with some descriptive adjectives.

2. **Write** Write a topic sentence. Then write a sentence for each fact on your list.

3. **Rewrite** Improve the paragraph. Combine short sentences into longer ones. Check to see that all the sentences are about the topic. Change the order of sentences if you wish.

4. **Edit** Check your spelling, punctuation, and word use. Make changes for your final copy.

EXAMPLE

Topic sentence
The coast was beautiful that July day.

Facts
1. big rocks in the water
2. cool summer breeze
3. waves on beach
4. white, sandy beach
5. clear, blue sea

Edited Paragraph

The coast was beautiful that July day. A summer breeze cooled us. We watched foamy waves roll onto the white, sandy beach. Tall, jagged rocks stood like towers in the clear, blue sea.

Activity A Use the steps in the writing process to write a paragraph that describes your favorite place. Write your paragraph on your paper.

Activity B Write a paragraph about George Washington. Use the following topic sentence and supporting facts and details:

Topic sentence
George Washington was a fine-looking man.
Facts and details
1. broad shoulders
2. 6 feet, 2 inches tall
3. stern look
4. blue-gray eyes
5. pale skin
6. stood straight

Activity C Write a paragraph that describes your dream house. What does it look like? What special features does it have? Be as creative as you wish. Use the steps in the writing process to write your paragraph.

Activity D Write a paragraph about a special moment in time. Use the steps in the writing process as you create a descriptive paragraph with the following information:

Topic sentence
The President of the United States was sworn into office.
Facts and details
1. on the steps of the Capitol in Washington, D.C.
2. big crowds watched
3. oath of office given by Chief Justice of the Supreme Court
4. new President made speech
5. crowd quiet, then loud cheering
6. cold day in January
7. before the long parade down Pennsylvania Avenue

Activity E Write a paragraph about the best or most important moment in your life. Use the steps in the writing process to write your paragraph.

Process paragraph

A paragraph that tells how something is done.

You can write a paragraph to explain how to do something. A **process paragraph** explains step-by-step how something is done. When writing a process paragraph, it is important to include each step of the process and to order the steps in the correct sequence.

1. **Prewrite** Think about a topic sentence. Jot it down. Add a list of steps.

2. **Write** Write a sentence for each step on your list. Keep your sentences about the steps short and easy to follow.

3. **Rewrite** Improve the paragraph. Check to see that you have not left out any steps. Be sure your sentences are in the right order.

4. **Edit** Check your spelling, punctuation, and word use. Make changes for your final copy.

EXAMPLE

Topic sentence

Bowling can be fun when you relax and follow these simple directions.

Steps

1. Hold the ball in front of you.
2. Take three steps toward the pins.
3. Roll the ball down the alley on your last step.

Edited paragraph

Bowling can be fun when you relax and follow a few simple directions. First, hold the ball in front of you. Next, take three steps toward the pins. Finally, roll the ball down the alley on your last step.

Activity A Write a process paragraph about sharpening a pencil.

Prewrite Watch someone sharpen a pencil. List each step. Then follow the rest of the writing process to complete your paragraph.

Activity B The steps in the following process paragraph are out of order. Put the steps in the correct order. Then rewrite the paragraph correctly on your paper.

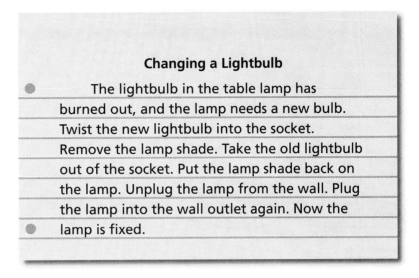

Changing a Lightbulb

The lightbulb in the table lamp has burned out, and the lamp needs a new bulb. Twist the new lightbulb into the socket. Remove the lamp shade. Take the old lightbulb out of the socket. Put the lamp shade back on the lamp. Unplug the lamp from the wall. Plug the lamp into the wall outlet again. Now the lamp is fixed.

Activity C Choose three of the following topics. On your paper, write a process paragraph about each topic. Be sure to follow the steps in the writing process.

Riding a Bicycle

Riding a Bicycle

Making a Sandwich

Selecting a Library Book

Dialing Long Distance

Washing the Dishes

Planting a Tree

Ironing a Shirt

Walking on Ice

Waxing a Car

Mowing the Lawn

Have you ever made up your mind to do something or believe something because you're sure that you are right? Then you read something that persuades you to change your mind. A **persuasive paragraph** tries to convince readers to think or act a certain way. When you write a persuasive paragraph, include language that will make people think and feel the way that you do about a topic.

Persuasive paragraph

A paragraph that tries to make readers believe something or do something.

1. **Prewrite** Jot down something you would like to persuade others to do. List reasons why others should believe the way you do about this topic.

2. **Write** Write a topic sentence that states your purpose (to persuade readers to do something). Then write sentences for each reason you listed.

3. **Rewrite** Check to see that you have listed all the reasons you can think of to support your topic. Change or add words that will make your paragraph more persuasive.

4. **Edit** Check your spelling, punctuation, and word use. Make changes for your final copy.

EXAMPLE   Allan's boss has decided to fire him to save the company money. Allan must persuade his boss not to fire him.

Topic sentence
I am a valuable worker for this company.

Facts
1) finish work on time
2) arrive on time
3) stay late sometimes
4) boss likes my work
5) work worth my pay

Edited paragraph
   I am a valuable worker for this company. I believe my work is worth the pay I receive. I always arrive at work on time; often, I stay late. My work is completed on time, and my boss likes the work I do. I believe I should continue working for this company.

Activity A Follow the directions to write a persuasive paragraph about why your friends should study with you tonight. Use the steps of the writing process to write your paragraph on your paper.

Prewrite Here are some possible reasons you might use to support the topic that you and your friends should study together. You can add reasons of your own.

• There is a test tomorrow.
• We can share ideas.
• We can read each other's notes.
• We can practice saying facts out loud.
• We can correct each other's work.

Write Use this topic sentence:

> Our group of friends should study together.

Activity B Rewrite and edit this persuasive paragraph to improve it. You may change the order of the sentences. You may combine sentences, and you may write additional sentences.

> My dog Buster is not dangerous. He has never bittes. He doesn't growls at peoples. He a friendly dog Buster likes peple. When he jumps up on people he's just saying helo. I keep Buster on a leash. When we walk But, it's not because he's a mean dog. very nice Every one likes Buster.

Activity C Choose three of these topics. Write a persuasive paragraph for each one.

1) Your favorite sports team is the best.
2) People should vote in elections.
3) Your town (or city or state) has more to offer than other places in the country.
4) Being a child (or teenager, young adult, senior citizen) is better than being any other age.
5) Regular exercise is important for good health.

Narrative

A series of paragraphs that go together to tell a story.

A **narrative** tells a story. A story has a series of paragraphs that tells what happens in the story. Notice how each paragraph in the following narrative helps to tell the story.

EXAMPLE **Mark's High-Wire Act**

1 Mark and his friend Dave went to the circus. A man in a satin suit walked on the high wire above the crowd. Mark thought this act looked easy.

2 The next morning, Mark stretched a wire across his backyard. "Anybody can do this," Mark said.

3 "A high-wire act is not easy," replied Dave.

4 Mark grabbed an umbrella and walked proudly to the wire. He put one foot on the wire. He felt like the man in the circus.

5 "Go, go!" Dave yelled. He clapped his hands and grinned.

6 Mark's foot shook. The wire shook. Mark shook. He waved his arms trying to keep his balance. He dropped the umbrella and fell to the ground.

7 Later, Mark said, "You were right, Dave. High-wire acts are for the circus. It's scary stuff. I'm still shaking!"

8 Dave laughed. "Your high-wire act was only a foot off the ground!" he said.

Activity A Write the answer to each question about the example narrative.

1) What paragraph introduces the story characters? What are the characters' names?

2) Where does most of the story take place? What paragraph tells you this?

3) What does Mark want to do? What does Dave say to try to get Mark to change his mind?

4) What paragraphs have descriptive details only and no words spoken by the characters?

5) Why does Dave laugh at the end?

One way writers make a story interesting is by using **dialogue.** Dialogue is conversation between two or more characters in a story. Dialogue helps readers get to know what the story characters are like and why they act the way they do. In a story, a new paragraph begins each time the speaker changes or when the topic changes.

Another way writers make a story interesting is by adding a twist at the end that surprises or shocks readers.

Activity B On your paper, list ways that the writer made "Mark's High-Wire Act" interesting for you.

Activity C Write the following as a story. Remember to begin a new paragraph each time the speaker changes.

> "Hi," said Vivian. "Well, hello," said Stan. "It's nice to see you again," said Vivian. "Thanks," said Stan. "I'm heading for the library," said Vivian. "Me, too," said Stan. "Let's stop for pizza on the way." "Great idea! I'm starving," said Vivian. "Maybe we could see a movie on the way home." Then Stan said, "Maybe we should skip the library and catch the early show."

Every story has a beginning, a middle, and an end. The beginning introduces the setting, the characters, and the main character's goal. The middle tells how the main character tries to achieve the goal. The end tells what happens to the main character when the goal is reached.

Activity D Here is the beginning of a story. Use the writing process to write a middle and an end. Be as creative as you can be.

> **The Gold Seeker**
>
> Each morning at sunrise, Jesse is at the creek. He dips his pan into the soft, sandy bottom. Slowly, he pours muddy water from his pan. His eyes and fingers search for specks of gold. Hours pass, and the sun burns his skin.
>
> One day . . .
>
> *What happens to Jesse? What does he do? Are any other people involved?*

Have you recently seen a movie that you really liked? Perhaps you saw a TV program that you disliked. Your ideas about a movie or a television program can be written as a **review.** A review tells one person's opinion about a movie, television program, play, or written work.

Review

A writer's opinion about a movie, TV show, book, or play.

1. **Prewrite** Think about something you read or saw recently. Jot it down. Did you like it or not? List your reasons for liking or disliking this work.

2. **Write** Write a topic sentence that states your opinion. Write a sentence for each supporting reason on your list.

3. **Rewrite** Improve the paragraph as you rewrite it.

4. **Edit** Correct your spelling, punctuation, and word use.

Read the nursery rhyme "Humpty Dumpty" and the two reviews that follow.

EXAMPLE

**Humpty Dumpty sat on a wall,
Humpty Dumpty had a great fall.
All the king's horses and all the king's men
Couldn't put Humpty together again.**

Topic sentences stating different opinions

1. "Humpty Dumpty" teaches about poetry and life.
2. "Humpty Dumpty" is a waste of a person's time.

Reasons

First opinion	Second opinion
nice sound	sad
good rhythm	violent
warns about being careful	no one could help

Edited paragraphs

1. The nursery rhyme "Humpty Dumpty" teaches about poetry and life. The poem sounds nice because it has good rhythm. It also warns about what can happen if you're not careful with your life.

2. The nursery rhyme "Humpty Dumpty" is a waste of a person's time. The poem is filled with sadness and violence. Humpty was hurt, and no one could help him. That's a very sad idea.

Do you remember what happens in the fairy tale "Little Red Riding Hood"? A little girl walks through the forest to her grandmother's house, bringing gifts. Her mother has told her not to stop to talk with anyone. She meets and talks with a wolf; she tells him that she is bringing a basket of goodies to her grandmother. The wolf runs ahead and eats the grandmother. When Little Red Riding Hood arrives at the house, the wolf is waiting for her. A hunter arrives, shoots the wolf, and saves the child.

In your opinion, is "Little Red Riding Hood" a good story for children? What does it teach? Is it too violent? Does it have any value?

Activity A On your paper, write a review of "Little Red Riding Hood." State your opinion clearly. Give at least three reasons for your opinion.

Activity B Write a review paragraph for one or more of these events.

1) A magic act   **5)** A club activity

2) A TV show   **6)** A sports activity

3) A lunchroom meal   **7)** A play

4) A class activity   **8)** A musical performance

Activity C Write a review about one or more of these topics.

1) A book you have read.

2) A poem you have read or heard.

3) A movie or TV show you have seen.

4) A computer program you have used.

5) A song you have sung or heard.

6) A favorite activity of your friends.

7) The efforts of your teachers to help you learn.

Body
The message part of a letter.

Closing
Word or phrase used before the signature in a letter.

Greeting
Word or words used before the name or title of the person to whom a letter is sent.

Heading
The address of the person writing a letter.

Signature
The name signed by the writer of a letter

You write friendly letters to people you know. Friendly letters share news about yourself and let people know you care about them.

Friendly letters follow a form that includes a **heading, greeting, body, closing,** and **signature**. The heading gives the address of the writer; it is followed by the date. The greeting addresses the person receiving the letter. *Dear Mary* is an example of a greeting. The body of the letter contains the message. The closing is a polite word or phrase that ends the letter. The signature is the name of the person writing the letter.

```
                          Heading _____
                          _____
                          Date _____


       Greeting _____ ,
       Body _____
       _____
       _____
       _____
       _____
       _____
       _____
       _____
       _____
       _____
       _____
       _____

                          Closing _____
                          Signature _____
```

Read the letter on the next page from Denise to her friend Estelle.

36 Center Street
Elkhart, Indiana 46517
March 17, 2001

Dear Estelle,

It's always nice to get a letter from you. I enjoy hearing about your school. Your new friends sound like nice people.

Your old friends here miss you. We often wish that you were here. We missed your help at the meeting last week. You have such good ideas.

The class is planning a trip to Washington, D.C., next month. Everybody is excited. We earned some money with car washes and bake sales. I hope you and I can meet when we are there since you live so close. I'll write again when I have more details, and we can make a plan.

My whole family is hoping you'll come for a visit this summer. We'd love to have you stay with us.

Sincerely,

Denise

Activity A On your paper, answer the following questions about Denise's letter.

1) What is Denise's address? Why is her address in the letter?

2) When did Denise write the letter?

3) What greeting does Denise use? What end punctuation mark follows the greeting?

4) What closing does Denise use? What end punctuation mark follows the closing?

5) How does Denise let Estelle know that she cares about her?

6) Why does Denise tell Estelle about the class trip?

Activity B Choose one idea below to write a letter. Use the correct letter form.

1) Pretend you are Estelle. Write a letter back to Denise.

2) Write a letter to a friend of your own.

It is important that you know how to address an envelope correctly. This will ensure that your letter reaches the person you are writing.

Put two addresses on the outside of an envelope. Print your return address in capital letters in the upper left-hand corner. Print the address of the person you are writing in capital letters in the center of the envelope. Usually, an address takes three lines. The person's title and name go on the first line. The street address goes on the second line. The city, state, and ZIP code go on the third line.

You may use the short form for state names, or you may use the full name. Be sure to print or type the entire address in capital letters. The U.S. Postal Service now uses machines to scan addresses on envelopes. Scanning machines look for capital letters and no punctuation, as shown in the following example.

> **EXAMPLE**
>
> MS DENISE AIELLO
> 36 CENTER STREET
> ELKHART IN 46517-2380
>
> Name: _____→ MS ESTELLE JOHNSON
> Street: _____→ 123 WEST MAIN AVENUE
> City, State ZIP Code: _____→ RESTON VA 22091-1234

Activity A On your paper, write each address as it should appear on an envelope. Look at the example above.

1) Dr. John Hall, 708 Terrace Drive, Columbus, Ohio 43201-5986

2) Mrs. Ellen Parker, 506 Allen Street, Vance, South Carolina 29163-6983

3) Dr. Rita Ponce, 48 Calle Rio, San Juan, Puerto Rico 00912-8255

4) Mr. Jack Perry, 16 Henry Place, Omega, Georgia 31775-3911

Activity B Match the words with their meanings. Write the number and its correct letter on your paper.

> **Words**
> **1)** paragraph
> **2)** topic sentence
> **3)** heading
> **4)** date
> **5)** closing
> **Meanings**
> **a)** goes in the upper right-hand part of a letter
> **b)** goes just above the signature
> **c)** group of sentences about one topic
> **d)** tells the main idea of a paragraph
> **e)** goes under the heading

Activity C Edit the following sentences. Write the edited sentences on your paper.

1) Bills house hasn't no yard

2) School start in a few week I hope I do good

3) I gets up early when I go to work tom said

4) Kelly wisht she had wait for her frend on main street

5) too baby lions arrived at the washington zoo arent they cute

6) that music is much too loud shouted tom

7) you're new computer program wont never fit this machine

8) watch you're steak on the grill its on fire steve yelled

9) my life here is empty im moving to detroit said susan to kerry

10) Mark didnt no which classes to choose for next yere

Part A "Rip Van Winkle" is a story about a man who slept for twenty years. When he woke, he found that many changes had taken place. Think about Rip Van Winkle's long sleep. For points 1–5, choose one of the following and follow the directions.

- Write a five-sentence paragraph to describe the things you might see if you fell asleep today and woke up in twenty years.

- Write a five-sentence paragraph that explains how to make a bed.

- Write a five-sentence letter to a friend about your long sleep.

Part B On your paper, write these sentences as a conversation between Joe and Tom. Remember the rules for punctuating dialogue and for beginning a new paragraph when the speaker changes.

6) hello joe said tom hi tom said joe

7) tom said i am moving to kansas city missouri

8) i will miss you said joe

9) we will still be friends tom said

10) i can visit you during summer vacation joe said

11) we can also write letters to each other said tom

Part C Write the answers for each item on your paper.

12) List the facts you need for a party invitation.

13) List the facts you need for a news story.

14) Write an envelope for a letter from you to Mr. John Smith, 112 Elm Street, Moscow, Idaho 83843-1334.

15) Write an envelope for a letter from you to Ms. Lenore Jones, 2345 River Drive, Clive, Iowa 50325-1269.

Part D Write a memo for this phone call. Include in your memo the six things listed.

> Saul called on October 15 at 5:15 P.M. He wants Ramone to call him about the time and place of the tennis tournament.

16) To   18) Subject   20) Time

17) From   19) Date   21) Message

Part E For points 22–26, write a five-sentence short story. Choose one of these two situations. Begin your story in a way that will capture readers' attention. Try to add a surprising twist at the end of your story.

- Casey is always jumping to the wrong conclusions. One day, he is standing in line at the bank. Suddenly, he notices two suspicious-looking characters, all dressed in black. They are peeking around the corner of the alley across the street. Are the men bank robbers? Should Casey alert the bank guard? What does Casey do?

- Clark enjoyed looking at stars and planets through his telescope. One night he heard a voice each time he looked at the planet Saturn. What does the voice say to Clark? What does Clark do? Who does he tell? What do his friends think? Do his friends believe him?

Part F Create a fictional character. For points 27–30, write a four-sentence paragraph describing the character. Tell what the character looks like and something he or she did. Try to make the character believable for readers.

Test Taking Tip   When taking a multiple-choice test, read every choice before you answer a question. Put a line through choices you know are wrong. Then choose the best answer from the remaining choices.

mispel	misspell
goverment	government
mouses	mice
sheeps	sheep
feild	field
peice	piece
safty	safety
aweful	awful

Chapter

12

Spelling

Do you have trouble spelling certain words correctly? Spelling words correctly can be a challenge for many people. Some English words have the same sounds but are spelled differently. Other words are not spelled the way they sound at all.

You can learn certain rules to help you spell most English words correctly. Some words, however, do not follow the rules. You will have to memorize their spellings.

In this chapter, you will study ways to help you spell better.

Goals for Learning

▶ To practice the spelling of common problem words

▶ To choose the correct spelling of words that sound alike

▶ To change the spelling of nouns to form plurals

▶ To practice spelling other word endings correctly

▶ To practice the use of *-ie* and *-ei*

The more you practice a skill, the easier that skill becomes. Spelling is a skill that takes practice. Focus your practice on words that give you trouble. Soon you will be able to spell those words with ease.

Here is one strategy, or method, you can use to practice spelling a new or difficult word.

1. Copy the word on your paper correctly.

2. Write the word again while you say it aloud.

3. Cover the word. Say it. Then write it as you spell it aloud.

4. Check your spelling. If the word is spelled incorrectly, return to steps 2 and 3.

The following words are often misspelled. You may find learning their spellings is easier if you study the words in small groups.

Group 1	Group 3	Group 5	Group 7	Group 9
accident	disturb	instead	once	speech
arctic	doctor	judge	paid	study
athletic	February	knock	pleasant	thought
beggar	finally	maybe	pretty	toward
beginning	forgot	minute	probably	trail
boundary	forty	misspell	review	trial

Group 2	Group 4	Group 6	Group 8	
calendar	fourteen	necessary	safety	
children	government	nickel	Saturday	
consider	grammar	nineteen	sentence	
curious	guard	ninety	shovel	
decide	history	occur	since	
destroy	hundred	often	speak	

Spelling

Activity A Find the misspelled word in each sentence. Write the word correctly on your paper.

1) The artic cold froze my toes.

2) Alec's car was in an acident, but he had the car fixed.

3) Our school has the best atletic teams in the state.

4) He was once a poor begger; now he's rich and famous.

5) This is the begining of a long movie.

6) The fence marks the boundry of our property.

7) Lots of childern play in the park during the summer.

8) The members of the jury will concider the case in private.

9) I was cureous about the contents of the big box in the basement.

10) The results of this test will diside my grade for the term.

Activity B Find the misspelled word in each sentence. Write the word correctly on your paper.

1) The raging fire will destory the forest lands.

2) My mother was quiet so she would not desturb my sleep.

3) I think you should call the docter if your fever goes any higher.

4) Valentine's Day is on Febuary 14th.

5) The letter from my best friend finaly arrived.

6) Over fourty people came to the big party.

7) My little sister will be forteen years old on her next birthday.

8) The members of our state goverment meet in the capitol building.

9) Sue earns high grades on her grammer tests.

10) Adam is in trouble; he fourgot his homework.

Homonym

A word that sounds like another word but has a different meaning and spelling.

Homonyms are words that sound alike but have different meanings and different spellings. You can figure out which homonym to use by thinking about the meaning of the other words in the sentence.

EXAMPLES

Homonyms		Definitions
been	(verb)	past form of *be*
bin	(noun)	a box used for storage
blue	(adjective)	a color; feeling sad
blew	(verb)	past form of *blow*
break	(verb)	to destroy
	(noun)	some time off
brake	(noun)	used to stop a car, bike, truck, or other vehicle
buy	(verb)	to pay for something
by	(preposition)	beside; near; within a certain time
dear	(adjective)	loved
deer	(noun)	animal
fair	(noun)	a show with amusements
	(adjective)	pleasing; average; just
fare	(noun)	the price of a ride
for	(preposition)	used to show the purpose or a reason
four	(noun)	a number

Activity A Write the homonym in parentheses that completes each sentence correctly.

1) Jake put trash in the (been, bin).

2) She has (been, bin) here before.

3) Jennifer has a new (blue, blew) bike.

4) The wind (blue, blew) hard all night.

5) Kerry feels (blue, blew) because her friend Susan is moving to Detroit.

6) Be careful, or you will (break, brake) the glass.

7) Put your foot on the (break, brake) right now and stop this car.

8) Juanita was tired, so she took a (break, brake) from her job.

9) The new calf stands (buy, by) its mother.

10) Derek will (buy, by) a new suit for his grandmother's birthday party.

11) His grandmother is a (dear, deer) person; everyone loves her.

12) The (dear, deer) are shy and run back into the woods whenever anyone comes near them.

13) We had (fair, fare) skies today with lots of sunshine.

14) Jill got on the bus and paid her (fair, fare).

15) Sarah won a blue ribbon for her apple pie at the county (fare, fair).

16) Karen said that she would be back home (buy, by) dinnertime.

17) That toy is very (dear, deer) to the little boy.

18) Do you think these new game rules are (fair, fare)?

19) Max bought (for, four) apples.

20) He wants a hot dog (for, four) lunch.

Activity B Rewrite and edit this paragraph. Correct the spelling, grammar, and punctuation. Try to improve the paragraph by adding words and combining ideas.

> Peg said It isnt fare I by a TV set it doesn't work I didn't brake it It just blue up buy the time I got back to the store it was close i went home and threw my new TV in the trash been. It just isnt fare.

Remember that homonyms are words that sound alike but have different meanings and spellings. To know which homonym to use in a sentence:

1. Think about the meaning of the other words in the sentence.

2. Think about the meaning of the homonyms.

3. Choose the homonym that makes sense in the sentence.

Practice using these homonyms in sentences.

EXAMPLES

Homonyms		Definitions
hear	(verb)	to listen to
here	(adverb)	this place
hoarse	(adjective)	harsh, scratchy
horse	(noun)	an animal
hour	(noun)	60 minutes; time
our	(pronoun)	belonging to us
knew	(verb)	past form of *know*; understood
new	(adjective)	recent; fresh
know	(verb)	to understand
no	(adjective)	not any
plain	(adjective)	not fancy
	(noun)	flat, wide-open land
plane	(noun)	airplane
so	(adverb)	very
	(conjunction)	in order that
sew	(verb)	to stitch cloth with thread
weather	(noun)	climate
whether	(conjunction)	if (used with *or*)

Activity A Write the homonym in parentheses that completes each sentence correctly.

1) She didn't (hear, here) me call her name.
2) (Hear, Here) is the money I owe you.
3) Anna will ride the black (hoarse, horse) to the ranch.
4) The coach's voice is (hoarse, horse) from yelling.
5) We met (hour, our) parents for dinner.
6) I'll meet you in one (hour, our).
7) I (knew, new) all the answers but one.
8) We moved into a (knew, new) house.
9) She does not (know, no) the answer to the last question.
10) We were late for dinner, and there was (know, no) food left.
11) They rode in a covered wagon across the grassy (plain, plane).
12) A small silver (plain, plane) landed at the airport.
13) Maria wore a (plain, plane) black dress to the party.
14) Tim baby-sat (sew, so) his parents could go out.
15) She will (sew, so) the tear in her pants.
16) I'm (so, sew) sorry you can't come with us to the movies.
17) He could not decide (weather, whether) he should go home early or stay late.
18) Today's (weather, whether) will be sunny and warm.

Activity B Rewrite and edit this paragraph. Correct the spelling, grammar, and punctuation. Try to improve the paragraph by adding words and combining ideas.

> it was the midle of the night I new there was something wrong. I could here the sound of a horse voice It was almost an our before I learnt the cause of the problem Hour knew neighbor has for big parrots and they talk to each other. Now that I no, I can sleep

Lesson 4 — Plurals—Two or More

Singular
One.

Plural
More than one.

A **singular** noun names one person, place, or thing. A **plural** noun names more than one person, place, or thing. Add *-s* or *-es* to most singular nouns to form their plurals.

EXAMPLES

Singular	Plural
car	cars
tire	tires
glass	glasses
dish	dishes

Activity A Write each singular noun on your paper. Beside each noun, write its plural.

1) hat
2) frog
3) fire
4) town
5) rock
6) school
7) building
8) truck
9) bike
10) road
11) box
12) pass
13) watch
14) bush
15) bus

To form the plural of most nouns that end in *-y*, change the *y* to *i* and add *-es*. Add *-s* to form the plural of nouns that end in a vowel plus *y*.

EXAMPLES

Singular	Plural
penny	pennies
boy	boys

Activity B Write each singular noun on your paper. Beside each noun, write its plural.

1) sky
2) toy
3) glossary
4) fly
5) lady
6) library
7) daisy
8) family
9) key
10) day
11) guy
12) bakery
13) copy
14) valley
15) monkey

Add -*s* to some words that end in -*f* or -*fe* to form their plurals. For other words that end in -*f* or -*fe*, change the *f* or *fe* to *v* and add -*es*.

EXAMPLES	Singular	Plural
	chief	chiefs
	knife	knives

Activity C Write each singular noun on your paper. Beside each noun, write its plural.

1) leaf **4)** loaf **7)** yourself

2) shelf **5)** thief **8)** wolf

3) calf **6)** half **9)** elf

Some nouns form their plurals in irregular ways. Some nouns do not change at all to form their plurals.

EXAMPLES	Singular	Plural
	child	children
	man	men
	woman	women
	foot	feet
	mouse	mice
	goose	geese
	tooth	teeth
	sheep	sheep
	deer	deer

Activity D Write each sentence correctly on your paper. Change the singular nouns in bold to plural nouns.

1) The two **man** were diving from **cliff.**

2) They hit the water between two **wave.**

3) Their **tooth** chattered from the cold.

4) **Tree** and **bush** lined the shore.

5) Three **child** each paid five **penny** to pet the **sheep.**

6) I read four **book** about **deer** this summer.

7) Both **library** are closed on **Sunday.**

8) The police **chief** met to talk about the **thief.**

You can add endings to many words to make new words. Follow these two spelling rules for adding endings to some words.

1. When adding an ending to a word that ends in -*e*, drop the final *e* if the ending starts with a vowel. Do not drop the *e* if the ending starts with a consonant.

EXAMPLES	love + less	=	loveless
	love + ly	=	lovely
	love + ing	=	loving
	love + able	=	lovable

2. When adding an ending that begins with a vowel to one-syllable words with a short vowel sound, double the final consonant before adding the ending.

EXAMPLES	stop + ed	=	stopped
	sit + ing	=	sitting

Some words do not follow the spelling rules. If you are not sure how to spell a word with an ending added, check the dictionary.

EXAMPLES	awe + ful	=	awful
	courage + ous	=	courageous
	fix + ing	=	fixing
	judge + ment	=	judgment

Activity A Add the endings to each of the following words. Write the new words on your paper. Follow the first spelling rule.

1) care + ful

2) care + ing

3) care + less

4) fame + ous

5) flame + less

6) prime + ary

7) safe + ty

8) bride + al

9) like + ly

10) like + ness

11) store + age

12) place + ment

Activity B Add the endings to each of the following words. Write the new words on your paper. Follow the second spelling rule.

1) flag + ed

2) hit + ing

3) hop + ing

4) let + ing

5) step + ed

6) spin + ing

7) slap + ing

8) shop + ed

9) rub + ing

10) win + er

11) fat + en

12) stir + ed

13) hot + est

14) sad + er

15) plan + ing

16) skip + ed

Activity C Rewrite and edit this paragraph. Correct the spelling, grammar, and punctuation. Try to improve the paragraph by adding words and combining ideas.

The bater steped to the plate he is planing on hiting a home run. The pitcher is rubing the ball. the pitcher is the hotest, fasttest player in the league. The ball is spining. The bater carefuly conects with the ball fans in the stands make an aweful noise. The ball skipps across the fence for a home run. It realy is a good game

Words with the vowel pairs *-ie* and *-ei* often cause spelling problems. Remember the following rules when spelling words with these vowel pairs. Notice that each rule has exceptions. Exceptions do not follow the rules.

● Write *-i* before *-e* when the vowel sound is long *e* except after the letter *c*.

EXAMPLES	believe	field	receive	deceit
exceptions	either	seize	weird	

● Write *-e* before *-i* when the vowel sound is not long *e*.

EXAMPLES	weigh	eight	forfeit	neighbor
exceptions	view	friend	conscience	

Activity A Fill in the blanks with *-ei* or *-ie*. Write the words on your paper.

1) rel_ _f
2) f_ _ld
3) rec_ _ve
4) n_ _ghbor
5) ch_ _f
6) dec_ _ve
7) pr _ _ st
8) rec_ _pt
9) gr_ _ve
10) n_ _ce
11) c_ _ling
12) l_ _sure
13) for_ _gn
14) bel_ _f
15) _ _ght

Activity B Find the misspelled words in these sentences. Write the words correctly on your paper. A sentence may have one or more mistakes.

1) Ken plays iether first base or right feild.

2) He has a batting avrage of .300.

3) Tom has been hiting the ball hard latly, to.

4) A fast inside patch nocked off his glases.

5) The picher through another fastball.

6) Ken told the coachs that he needed some releif as he droped his bat.

7) Woodcrest is one of the busyest towns in the whole state.

8) People try seting new records buy doing some very wierd things.

9) Dennis swated too flys at one time.

10) Alice went to three scools last year because her famaly moved so offen.

11) The docter said that Jane's wisdom tooths had to be pulled.

12) Hour neighbor's dog just gave birth to ieght of the cutest little puppys you ever saw.

13) Tony gave Sara advise about her studys.

14) Wendy is learning a foriegn language.

15) He recieved the funnyest letter from his neice.

16) Six mouses made a nest behind the stove.

17) The mans made lunchs for thier wifes every day.

18) Rod selected a stack of books for liesure reading.

19) Suri holds strong believes about that topic.

20) I read an aweful reveiw of his lattest play.

Some words with similar spelling patterns and similar sounds can cause spelling problems. These words are often confused. Be careful when using them.

EXAMPLES

Words		Definitions
already	(adverb)	by this time
all ready	(adjective)	prepared
breath	(noun)	air
breathe	(verb)	to inhale and exhale air
close	(verb)	shut
	(adjective)	near; dear
clothes	(noun)	things to wear
cloths	(noun)	pieces of fabric
dairy	(noun)	shop where milk products are sold
diary	(noun)	daily record or journal
desert	(noun)	land without water
	(verb)	to leave alone
dessert	(noun)	last course of a meal; sweets
loose	(adjective)	free; not held tightly
lose	(verb)	to misplace; to fail to win
quiet	(adjective)	not noisy
quit	(verb)	to stop or leave
quite	(adverb)	completely; rather

Activity A Write the word or words in parentheses that complete each sentence correctly.

1) We've packed our things, and we're (already, all ready) for our trip.

2) The train was (already, all ready) at the station when we got there.

3) I cannot hold my (breath, breathe) for very long.

4) Open your mouth and (breath, breathe) in the fresh, country air.

5) Please (close, clothes, cloths) the window.

6) You can dust the furniture with one of the old dusting (close, clothes, cloths).

7) Don't sit too (close, clothes, cloths) to the open window.

8) Rosa will need all new (close, clothes, cloths) for work.

9) Brittany writes in her (dairy, diary) every night.

10) I bought some ice cream at the (dairy, diary).

11) I served the ice cream for (desert, dessert).

12) I prefer the dry (desert, dessert) air to the hot, humid air on the coast.

13) I would never (desert, dessert) you in your time of need.

14) He will (loose, lose) his job if business doesn't pick up soon.

15) The clown's pants were so (loose, lose) they kept falling down.

16) Be (quiet, quit, quite) and don't make a sound.

17) There is nothing (quiet, quit, quite) as refreshing as a morning swim in the sea.

18) Ben will (quiet, quit, quite) his job if he does not get a raise.

Activity B Rewrite and edit this paragraph. Correct the spelling, grammar, and punctuation. Try to improve the paragraph by adding words and combining ideas.

> The diner is quite this time of day In the evening it is quit busy and noisy. Jean and Al are clothes freinds. They often meets for lunch. Jean had all ready eaten when Al came in wearing new close. Jean was having fruit for desert. She keeps a dairy abot what she eats. She writes in it evry day. She does not need to loose wait she just wants to eat healthy foods

Adverbs can compare when, where, and how things happen. Add *-er* to an adverb to compare one thing to one other thing. Add *-est* to an adverb to compare two or more things.

EXAMPLES	Adverb	Comparing With One	Comparing With Two or More
	hard	harder	hardest
	fast	faster	fastest

Some adverbs change their form to make comparisons. The adverb *well* means "in the right way." Don't confuse the adverb *well* with the adjective *good*.

EXAMPLE	Adverb	Comparing With One	Comparing With Two or More
	well	better	best

Activity A On your paper, write the correct form of the adverb in parentheses to complete each sentence.

1) Andy played (good, well) in the first quarter.

2) He played a little (better, best) in the second quarter.

3) He played (better, best) of all at the end of the game.

4) Amy did (good, well) in math on Monday.

5) Her friend did (better, best) than she did on Tuesday.

6) Amy studied hard and did (better, best) of all the students on Friday.

Use *more* and *most* and *less* and *least* to make comparisons with adverbs that end in *-ly*.

EXAMPLES	Adverb	Comparing With One	Comparing With Two or More
	happily	more happily less happily	most happily least happily
	quickly	more quickly less quickly	most quickly least quickly
	quietly	more quietly less quietly	most quietly least quietly

Activity B Write the correct form of the adverb in parentheses to complete each sentence.

1) Mario's new car runs (more, most) efficiently than his old car.

2) It reaches 70 miles per hour (more, most) quickly than his old car.

3) It burns oil (less, least) rapidly than his old car, too.

4) Mario's friends like his old car, but they like his new car (better, best).

5) Beth finishes her homework (faster, fastest) than I do.

6) Of all the teams in the league, our team worked (harder, hardest).

7) Joanna works (more, most) happily at her job than Ellie does.

8) Paul moves swiftly; Josh moves (more, most) swiftly.

9) When the four team members ran around the track, Brenda ran the distance (more, most) easily.

10) Jack handles eggs (more, most) carefully than he handles bread.

11) She sings (more, most) clearly of all the members of the group.

12) Of all their children, Pete speaks (more, most) softly.

Part A Change the nouns in bold to plural nouns. Write the plural nouns on your paper.

1) Behind the barn, two **calf** chewed on some **bush.**

2) Inside the barn, **mouse** sank their **tooth** into stray **kernel** of corn.

3) **Fly** buzz.

4) Farm **child** ride **bus** to their **school.**

5) **Day** go by, and the **leaf** turn red and yellow.

6) During the summer, the lake is full of **goose.**

7) The man at the circus threw **knife** at his partner.

8) The **monkey** climbed to the top of the **tree.**

9) Lance checked both **library** and made several **copy** of his **note.**

10) Beyond those **hill** lie two large **valley.**

Part B Write the word in parentheses that is spelled correctly.

11) Craig and Lucy had an (arguement, argument) about TV shows.

12) Anton's two sisters (skiped, skipped) rope in the park.

13) Sharon thought the computer game was (awful, aweful).

14) "What a (lovly, lovely) idea," said Ruth.

15) At the party, Zoe saw three (famous, fameous) people.

Part C Write the word in parentheses that is spelled correctly.

16) (Either, Iether) we go to the movies now or we go later.

17) As a boy, Mr. Edwards was always into (mischeif, mischief).

18) The walls are white and the (cieling, ceiling) is blue.

19) The (doctor, docter) took blood from Allen's (vien, vein).

20) Tammy will (recieve, receive) a letter from her (friend, freind) soon.

Part D Rewrite the paragraph. Choose the word in parentheses that is spelled correctly and that completes the sentence correctly.

Adam and Caroline traveled west **21)** (threw, through) the hot **22)** (desert, dessert). **23)** (Sum, Some) **24)** (families, familys) in the wagon train were **25)** (weak, week) from hunger and thirst. Adam had shot **26)** (dear, deer) in the forests, but he **27)** (new, knew) few wild animals were **28)** (hear, here).

The **29)** (skies, skys) were clear. **30)** (Their, There) was no **31)** (break, brake) in the heat during the **32)** (dais, days). Later, at the water **33)** (whole, hole), **34)** (their, there) was **35)** (piece, peace) and **36)** (quite, quiet) among the **37)** (hoarses, horses).

At night, the travelers **38)** (heard, herd) **39)** (wolfs, wolves) beyond the light of their campfires. The sleep of these **40)** (mans, men) and women was **41)** (breif, brief), and they were **42)** (carful, careful) about their **43)** (safety, safty). At least, they **44)** (received, recieved) cool night air for **45)** (relief, releif).

Test Taking Tip

After you have completed a test, reread each question and answer. Ask yourself: Have I answered the question that was asked? Is my answer complete?

Chapter

13

Fine-Tuning Your Writing

L ook around you. Is there something you would like to change or improve? Perhaps you can brighten up your room with new wallpaper or a fresh coat of paint. It might help to rearrange the furniture. Maybe you can hang a colorful poster or an interesting photograph on the wall. Is your car in good shape? It might work better and run more smoothly if it had a tune-up. A wax and polish could make it shine.

You can fine-tune your writing so that it works better and flows more smoothly. Changing words and adding details can make your sentences more interesting. Rearranging sentences in a paragraph can make your ideas easier to follow and understand. Correcting mistakes in punctuation, spelling, and grammar will add polish to your writing and make it shine.

In this chapter, you will practice ways to improve your writing.

Goals for Learning

▶ To make subjects agree with verbs and pronouns agree with nouns

▶ To identify improperly written sentences

▶ To rewrite sentences to improve them

▶ To avoid the use of nonstandard English

▶ To use standard English to speak and to write

You have learned that every sentence has a subject and a verb. The rule of **agreement** states that a verb must agree in number with its subject. A singular subject takes a singular verb. A plural subject takes a plural verb.

Agreement

The rule that a singular subject has a singular verb, and a plural subject has a plural verb.

EXAMPLES	Singular:	He eats.
	Plural:	They eat.
	Singular:	Maria plays the piano.
	Plural:	The two girls play the piano.
	Singular:	The rabbit runs fast.
	Plural:	Rabbits run fast.

Do not be confused by plural nouns in titles. The title of a book, poem, song, movie, or play is singular.

EXAMPLE   *Invaders From Planet Worm* is a silly movie.

(Although *invaders* is a plural noun, the subject *Invaders From Planet Worm* names one movie. The singular subject takes the singular verb *is*.)

Do not be confused by plural nouns in phrases, clauses, or appositives that come between the subject and verb.

EXAMPLES   The **mother** of my two best friends **teaches** Spanish at our school.

(*Mother* is the singular subject. It takes the singular verb *teaches*.)

A **box** that contains glass bottles **falls**.

(*Box* is the singular subject. It takes the singular verb *falls*.)

The **boy**, one of three winners, **smiles** proudly for the camera.

(*Boy* is the singular subject. It takes the singular verb *smiles*.)

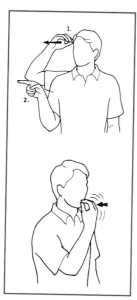

He eats.

Activity A Copy the sentences on your paper. Underline the subject and circle the complete verb. Then write whether the subject and verb are *singular* or *plural*.

1) A small child plays with the toy.

2) The group of children gets on the bus.

3) Several geese are flying over the field.

4) His store, which sells chairs, opens for business today.

5) Two teachers from our school play in a rock band.

6) Alice, a swim teacher for young children, works for the town.

7) *Raiders of the Lost Ark* stars Harrison Ford.

8) Sheep from Ted's ranch graze on the grassy hill.

Activity B Write the verb in parentheses that agrees with the subject.

1) A woman with twin boys (buy, buys) a dozen eggs.

2) The eggs (come, comes) from a local farm.

3) A hen (lays, lay) an egg.

4) Many hens (lays, lay) eggs.

5) A chicken (clucks, cluck).

6) A farmer (collects, collect) the eggs.

7) Farmers (sells, sell) the eggs to grocery stores.

8) Then farmers (buys, buy) more feed for their chickens.

Activity C Rewrite and edit this paragraph. Correct the agreement of subjects and verbs. Improve the sentences by combining them or changing their order.

> The roads across America is busy. Vehicles of all kinds drives on the highways. A trip to distant places are fun for families. People likes all the parks and beach and mountain in our country Some national parks has a few wolf and bear. When people respects wildlife, all living things is safe. Then people enjoys the outdoor life.

You can avoid common mistakes with subject-verb agreement if you keep the following rules in mind.

- A compound subject always takes a plural verb. Pay careful attention when the first part of a compound subject is plural and the second part is singular.

> **EXAMPLES**   The **choir** and the **band are** performing.
> The **boys** and their **sister sing** well.

- In a sentence that begins with the adverb *here* or *there*, the subject follows the verb. Find the subject. If the subject is singular, it takes a singular verb. If the subject is plural, it takes a plural verb.

> **EXAMPLES**   Singular: There **goes** a very large **truck**.
> Plural: There **go** three very large **trucks**.

- In a question, the subject often follows the verb or comes between the helping verb and main verb. Find the subject. If the subject is singular, it takes a singular verb. If the subject is plural, it takes a plural verb.

> **EXAMPLES**   Singular: **Is** your **sister** coming with us?
> Plural: Where **are** the **boy** and his **dog**?
> Plural: **Do** the **girls know** the words to the song?

Activity A Write each sentence. Underline the subject. Choose the verb in parentheses that agrees with the subject.

1) Louis and Tim (is, are) in the choir.
2) (Do, Does) the members of the choir sing this Saturday?
3) Louis and Tim (have, has) been singing in the choir for five years.
4) The band and the choir (was, were) on television.

5) Here (come, comes) Mr. Whithall, the band leader.

6) When (is, are) the choir and band practicing?

7) The choir and the band (travel, travels) to other towns.

8) The choir members and their leader (has, have) a picnic in June.

9) There (go, goes) the buses with the choir members and the band.

10) Where (is, are) the bus with all of the food?

11) (Is, Are) the families of the choir members invited?

12) The choir members, their leader, and their families (has, have) fun together.

Activity B Write the verb in parentheses that agrees with the subject.

1) Here (come, comes) the winning team.

2) There (stand, stands) the tallest statue in the city.

3) Here (is, are) your test scores.

4) (Is, Are) there many cars and trucks on the highways?

5) There (has, have) been several accidents this winter.

6) There (was, were) some people stranded by the storm.

7) (Is, Are) more snow in the weather forecast?

8) There (is, are) several large motels in the next town.

9) There (is, are) one motel with a good restaurant.

10) (Do, Does) your family and friends eat there?

Activity C Rewrite and edit this paragraph. Correct the agreement of subjects and verbs. Improve the sentences by combining them or changing their order.

> Here is my friends. Here is the place where we has parties. There are the table for snacks. Here come more friends. There is a big crowd now. Are there enough food? Is there too many people? Are there room for everyone? Well, we always has good times together.

Some pronouns that refer to people and things in general are always singular. Some are always plural. Remember that a singular subject takes a singular verb. A plural subject takes a plural verb.

Singular		Plural
anybody	everything	both
anyone	neither	few
each	no one	many
either	nobody	others
everybody	somebody	several
everyone	someone	

EXAMPLES   Singular: Does anybody want pizza?
Plural: Many want pizza.

Some pronouns that refer to people and things in general can be both singular or plural. These are:

all	any	most	none	some

If the noun that the pronoun refers to is singular, the pronoun is singular. If the noun is plural, the pronoun is plural.

EXAMPLES   Singular: Most of the pizza has been eaten.
Plural: Most of the pizzas have been eaten.

The singular pronouns *everybody, everyone,* and *everything* cause special problems with subject-verb agreement. Try to think of each of these words as a group. A noun that names a group usually takes a singular verb.

EXAMPLES   Everyone is hungry.
Everybody wants pizza.
Everything on the pizzas was fresh.

Activity A Write each sentence. Underline the subject. Choose the verb in parentheses that agrees with the subject.

1) Several (stand, stands) in line.

2) Few (leave, leaves) the line.

3) No one (is, are) pushing and shoving.

4) Many (wait, waits) for hours.

5) Each of the women (get, gets) concert tickets.

6) Others in line (is, are) not so lucky.

7) Everyone (want, wants) tickets for the show.

8) Neither of the lines (is, are) shorter than the other.

9) Somebody (tell, tells) a joke.

10) (Does, do) anyone look unhappy?

11) Everybody from our group (has, have) a ticket now.

12) Both (see, sees) the stage well.

13) One of the actors (have, has) forgotten his lines.

14) Everything (has, have) gone wrong for him tonight.

Activity B Write each sentence. Underline the subject. Choose the verb in parentheses that agrees with the subject.

1) Several of the choir members (was, were) practicing.

2) (Have, Has) any of the members gone home yet?

3) None of that song (sound, sounds) good.

4) All of the singers (was, were) tired.

5) Each of the farmer's fields (need, needs) extra work.

6) Most of the work (has, have) been finished.

7) Some of the dogs (is, are) barking.

8) Nobody in the barns (know, knows) about the cattle contest.

9) (Do, Does) anybody know the words to this song?

10) There (is, are) some of the sandwich left for you.

An owner pronoun and the noun it refers to should agree in number and gender.

> **EXAMPLES**   **Lynda** hooked **her** rope to the cliff.
>
> (The pronoun *her* refers to the singular feminine noun, *Lynda.*)
>
>   **Josh** and **Brenda** hooked **their** ropes to the cliff.
>
> (The pronoun *their* refers to the compound subject *Josh* and *Brenda.* A compound subject is plural so the pronoun is plural.)
>
>   **Each** of the men took **his** car to Sam's station.
>
> (The pronoun *his* refers to the singular pronoun *each.* The masculine form is used because *each* refers to *men,* a masculine noun that is the object of the preposition *of.*)

If you are not sure whether you should use *her* or *his,* try these choices.

- Use both *his* and *her.*
- Reword the sentence.
- Do not use a pronoun at all.

> **EXAMPLES**   Each child liked his or her ice cream.
>   The children liked their ice cream.
>   Each child liked the ice cream.

Activity A Write each sentence with an owner pronoun. Underline the word to which the pronoun refers.

1) Brenda sprained _____ ankle.

2) I gave Brenda _____ help.

3) Together, we made _____ way down the cliff.

4) Josh called home on _____ cellular phone.

5) Kevin, Josh, and Brenda remember _____ day on the mountain.

6) Will you loan _____ car to Kevin?

A compound subject connected by *and* is plural. It takes a plural verb. A compound subject connected by *or* can be singular or plural.

> **EXAMPLES**
> Plural: Otis and Lee **work** here.
> Singular: Otis or Lee **works** here.
> Plural: Her sisters or her brothers **work** here.

Follow these rules when using the conjunctions *either-or* or *neither-nor* to connect compound subjects.

- If both parts of a compound subject are singular, use a singular verb.

> **EXAMPLES**
> **Either** Jan **or** Hank **is** singing tonight.
> **Neither** Jan **nor** Hank **is** singing tonight.

- If both parts of a compound subject are plural, use a plural verb.

> **EXAMPLES**
> **Either** the twins **or** their friends **are** singing.
> **Neither** the twins **nor** their friends **are** singing.

- If one part of a compound subject is singular and the other part is plural, the verb usually agrees with the part closest to the verb.

> **EXAMPLES**
> **Either** the twins **or** Jan **is** singing.
> **Neither** Jan **nor** the twins **are** singing.
> Jan **or** the twins **are** singing.

Activity B Write the verb in parentheses that agrees with the subject.

1) Either an onion or spices (is, are) in the stew.
2) Neither wolves nor tigers (live, lives) in that country.
3) Neither science nor math (is, are) my favorite subject.
4) Either tools or a flashlight (fit, fits) into the space.
5) Neither the women nor Chuck (know, knows) the way.
6) Either a burger or hot dogs (taste, tastes) good to me.
7) Neither Ron nor his friends (was, were) hungry.

You can avoid problems using *doesn't* and *don't* if you remember these things.

- *Doesn't* is a contraction for *does not*. *Does* and *doesn't* are used with singular subjects except *I* and *you*.

- *Don't* is a contraction for *do not*. *Do* and *don't* are used with plural subjects.

EXAMPLES

Singular	Plural
Mary **doesn't** swim.	Mary and Lee **don't** swim.
The cat **doesn't** swim.	The cats **don't** swim.
I **don't** swim.	We **don't** swim.
Don't you swim?	You two **don't** swim.

Activity A Complete each sentence with *don't* or *doesn't*. Write the sentences on your paper.

1) You _____ need money at the picnic.

2) She _____ look very tall.

3) They _____ want any dinner.

4) It _____ look good to me.

5) He _____ say very much.

6) We _____ play video games at the mall.

7) A hot summer _____ seem short.

8) Sandy and Ed _____ own a fax machine.

9) A pleasant vacation _____ seem long.

10) It _____ matter.

11) Grass and flowers _____ grow well in this dry climate.

12) A big truck _____ stop fast.

13) They _____ live in this town.

14) He _____ go to this school.

15) _____ she want ice cream?

Keep these rules in mind when using the pronouns *this,
that, these,* and *those.* Remember that *this, that, these,* and
those can also be used as adjectives.

- Use *doesn't* with *this* and *that.*
- Use *don't* with *these* and *those.*

Activity B Complete each sentence with *don't* or *doesn't.*
Write the sentences on your paper.

1) This book _____ belong to me.

2) That one _____ belong to me, either.

3) These _____ look good.

4) Those _____ look very good, either.

5) This _____ look much better.

6) _____ that seem like a good idea?

7) This room _____ look good.

8) That lamp _____ work.

9) These drapes _____ go with the sofa.

10) That carpet _____ go with anything.

11) Those pictures _____ hang straight.

12) These tables _____ match each other.

13) That window _____ open easily.

14) _____ those pillows look nice on the sofa?

15) _____ that plant have pretty flowers?

Activity C Rewrite and edit this paragraph. Correct the
agreement of subjects and verbs. Improve the sentences by
combining them or changing their order.

> My computer don't work good. Either the
> program or the machine aren't working right.
> When I call a repair service, they doesn't know
> nothing. My computer teacher at school help me.
> Now my computer do work. My printer are
> jammed. Neither my teacher nor my friends
> knows about that problem.

The meaning of an entire sentence can change when a word or a phrase is shifted. Read over your sentences. Be sure the sentence means what you want it to mean.

EXAMPLES Mary **just** met Leon at the party.

(Here *just* tells when Mary met Leon at the party. *Just* now.)

Mary met **just** Leon at the party.

(Here *just* tells who Mary met at the party. She met *just* Leon and no one else.)

Only Matt knows the third answer.

(Here *only* means no one but Matt knows the third answer.)

Matt knows **only** the third answer.

(Here *only* means Matt knows the third answer, but he does not know any other answers.)

Matt knows the **only** answer.

(Here *only* means there is one answer, and Matt knows it.)

Activity A On your paper, explain the difference in meaning between the sentences in each group.

1) Only Jenny looked at the birthday cake.
Jenny looked only at the birthday cake.
Jenny looked at the only birthday cake.

2) Sarah just suggested that Jenny cut a slice.
Sarah suggested that Jenny cut just a slice.

3) I just brought in the CD player.
I brought in just the CD player.

4) Dee earned just twenty dollars.
Just Dee earned twenty dollars.
Dee just earned twenty dollars.

5) That bank stays open late only on Thursdays.
Only that bank is open late on Thursdays.

6) Only Beth, Dee's friend, wants a job at the bank.
Dee's only friend, Beth, wants a job at the bank.
Dee's friend Beth wants a job only at the bank.

Try to place phrases close to the words they describe. A sentence may not make sense or its meaning may be unclear if a phrase is misplaced.

EXAMPLES

Unclear: The women talked about flower gardens **at work**.

(Did the gardens grow at work? Probably not.)

Clear: The women talked **at work** about flower gardens.

Unclear: The girl saw a monkey **on the way home**.

(Was the monkey on the way home? It's not likely.)

Clear: **On the way home**, the girl saw a monkey.

Activity B Find the misplaced phrase in each sentence. Rewrite the sentence so that its meaning is clear.

1) A package was mailed by Alice in brown paper.

2) Mom drove Gina home before dark in her car.

3) The children told stories about fish in the hall.

4) A stray cat wandered into the school with a fluffy tail.

5) The animals looked at me in the zoo through the bars.

6) The rabbit hid under the truck with the little white tail and long ears.

7) The bell rang for the start of the meeting in the tower.

8) The elephant sprayed the man in the car with a trunkful of water.

9) The people waited beside the buses with suitcases.

10) Karen went to the dance with Steve in a pretty dress.

You probably speak differently to your teachers and your boss than you do to your friends. Most people tend to use a more relaxed form of the English language when speaking to family and friends. In some cases, however, this relaxed attitude results in dialogue that has little or no meaning for listeners.

EXAMPLES "Well, I'd like this job and, well, I think you should hire me and, well, I hope you will."

"So, like, if you hire me and, like, I'm sick, like, do I get, like, sick leave?"

"You know, I think we need longer, you know, breaks, you know, because, you know, we're on our feet, you know, all day."

The repetition of *well*, *like*, and *you know* in the examples gets in the way of each speaker's message. Notice how the removal of these words makes the speaker's meaning clear.

EXAMPLES "I'd like this job, and I think you should hire me. I hope you will."

"If you hire me, and I get sick, do I get sick leave?"

"I think we need longer breaks because we're on our feet all day."

The English language is sometimes divided into two types.

1. Standard English is the English you read in most textbooks and hear on television and radio news programs. Standard English follows the rules of English grammar. It is always acceptable and correct.

2. Nonstandard English is the English you may use with your friends. You may also hear it spoken by characters in television shows and movies. Writers may use it in dialogue to make their characters sound like real people. Nonstandard English follows current styles of speech. It often contains slang and regional expressions. It does not always follow the rules of grammar. For these reasons, it is not acceptable to use nonstandard English in formal situations.

Here are examples of standard and nonstandard English.

EXAMPLES

Standard English	Nonstandard English
She isn't here.	She ain't here.
Where were you?	Where were you at?
Josh did well.	Josh done good.
He might have done it.	He might of done it.
She will try to go.	She will try and go.
He's been everywhere.	He's been everywheres.
Sam went all the way down the road.	Sam went a ways down the road.

Activity A Read what Pam tells her friend Beth about Ben, who works with her. Rewrite Pam's dialogue on your paper. Use standard English.

> I saw Ben in Shipping. So I go, "Hi," and he goes, "Hi yourself." Then he goes, "How you doing?" and I go, "Not bad. How about you?" So he goes, "Okay, sorta. I'm sorta hanging loose between things."

Activity B On your paper, rewrite the following dialogue. Use standard English.

> Colleen has done collected dolls from all over the world. She says, "I ain't never gonna stop. Like, I like dolls from everywheres on earth."
>
> Then I says, "Where did you find this one at?"
>
> Then she says, "Like, you know, in a store in New York. It's from like Tibet."
>
> Then I says, "I should of started a doll collection, too."
>
> Then she says, "I ain't too busy to try and help you."
>
> Then I says, "Thanks. You done real good with your set."

Good writers may edit and rewrite a story or an article several times before they feel satisfied. The edit and rewrite stages of the writing process are important and should never be rushed or skipped.

Activity A Read the first draft of a letter by an unhappy worker to her boss. On your paper, rewrite the paragraph to improve it. Use standard English. Correct mistakes in grammar, spelling, and punctuation.

> I got several problems with my job I ain't had enough time to do it right. I got too much to do. I beleive I need more time to complete this job well. Maybe two more weeks. I can do it, but I needs more time. I no the company wants good work and like I wants more time so's its done good.

Activity B Write the verb in parentheses that agrees with the subject.

1) "Memories" (is, are) a nice song.

2) Memories (is, are) nice.

3) "Big City Blues" (is, are) a sad piece of music.

4) (Have, Has) you heard the album?

5) *Happy Guys* (was, were) a funny movie.

6) The happy guys (was, were) played by good actors.

Activity C Match the words with their meanings. Write the number and its correct letter on your paper.

Words	Meanings
1) several	**a)** follows current styles of speech
2) everybody	**b)** names one group
3) agree	**c)** names more than one
4) standard English	**d)** follows rules of grammar in writing and speaking
5) nonstandard English	**e)** what subjects and verbs need to do

Try to avoid using sentences that ask *where* someone or something is located with the word *at*.

> **EXAMPLES** Nonstandard English: She knows where it's at.
> Standard English: She knows where it is.
> Nonstandard English: Where is the paper at?
> Standard English: Where is the paper?

Activity D Rewrite these sentences on your paper. Use standard English.

   1) I know where it's at.

   2) Where you been at?

   3) Let me know where you're at tonight.

   4) Tell me where Joe's going to be at tomorrow.

   5) Look where I'm at now!

   6) Where are you at with your homework?

   7) If you want good music, K101 is where it's at.

   8) Where have Ben and Todd been at lately?

   9) Where have you been at while I was gone?

   10) How can I know where you're at if you don't call?

Activity E Edit and rewrite these sentences. Use standard English.

   1) I ain't never been nowhere in my life.

   2) I'm like, "Where you at?"

   3) He don't go there no more.

   4) So I go, "No way! I ain't doing that!"

   5) We doesn't set on the porch no more.

Activity F Write five sentences that contain examples of nonstandard English. Then write each sentence in standard English.

Part A Write the verb in parentheses that agrees with the subject.

1) Bill and Jenny (is, are) two old friends.
2) They (have, has) flown jets for several years.
3) Both (are, is) checked out for carrier landings.
4) They often (lands, land) at night when the sea (is, are) rough.
5) Bill and Jenny (do, does) most of their flying together.
6) Their teamwork (have, has) earned them a fine military record.

Part B Copy each sentence. Underline each subject. Choose the correct form of the verb. Do not be confused by nouns in prepositional phrases.

7) Someone (has, have) answered all the questions.
8) Others (has, have) not finished the test.
9) Most (study, studies) hard for that class.
10) Many (earn, earns) good grades.
11) Each member of our class (take, takes) three tests today.
12) All of the tests (is, are) an hour long.
13) One of the tests (cover, covers) science.
14) The others (is, are) for math and English.
15) Rod and his friends (learn, learns) what the teacher expects from the class.
16) Everyone (like, likes) Andy's grill.
17) Each of the cooks (is, are) trained well.
18) One of the cooks (make, makes) great burgers.
19) Another cook (bake, bakes) hot rolls.
20) No one (complain, complains) about this food.

Part C Rewrite these sentences correctly on your paper.

21) tonys computer ain't new no more but it works good

22) his friend jill says that surfing the internet is fun but shes never sure where shes at

23) tony says your right that its fun but i doesn't have no modem

24) by one of them modems at the big store next to the park with the red neon sign said jill

25) their like easy to use said jill.

26) she said that alls you have to do is plug it in

27) the computer recieves all them signals jill told tony

28) the modem like sets on you're desk jill said and well the wires lies on the floor."

29) tony said i no where the store's at

30) I'm gonna get me one tomorrow he added

Part D Write the pronoun in parentheses that agrees with the subject.

31) One of the men has (his, their) own service station.

32) Sam keeps (his, its) station clean.

33) Few of the customers take (his, their) business anywhere else.

34) Each of the customers gave (her, their) thanks for the good job the men did.

35) Most of the people in town give (his, their) support to local businesses.

Test Taking Tip Review your corrected tests. You can learn from your own mistakes.

Glossary

Abbreviation—short form of a word (p. 194)

Abstract noun—a word that names something that cannot be seen or touched (p. 77)

Action verb—a word that tells what the subject of a sentence does (p. 10)

Adjective—a word that describes a noun (p. 8)

Adjective object complement—an adjective that adds meaning to the direct object (p. 118)

Adjective prepositional phrase—a prepositional phrase that describes a noun (p. 30)

Adjective subject complement—a word in the predicate that describes the subject (p. 136)

Adverb—a word that describes a verb, an adjective, or another adverb (p. 12)

Adverb prepositional phrase—a prepositional phrase that describes a verb (p. 34)

Agreement—the rule that a singular subject has a singular verb, and a plural subject has a plural verb (p. 262)

Appositive—a word or group of words that follows a noun and explains the noun or gives another name to the noun (p. 122)

Apostrophe (')—a punctuation mark in an owner's name (p. 94)

Article—a word that points out a noun (p. 9)

Body—the message part of a letter (p. 234)

Capital letter—a letter that is uppercase. *A* is a capital or uppercase letter; *a* is a lowercase letter (p. 4)

Capitalize—to use capital letters (p. 86)

Closing—word or phrase used before the signature in a letter (p. 234)

Colon (:)—a punctuation mark used in time (p. 194)

Comma (,)—a punctuation mark used to set apart one or more words (p. 22)

Common noun—the name of a general type of person, place, or thing (p. 44)

Comparative—an adjective that compares two nouns (p. 152)

Complete predicate—the whole part of a sentence that tells what the subject is doing (p. 18)

Complete subject—the whole part of a sentence that tells who or what the sentence is about (p. 18)

Complex sentence—a sentence that includes both an independent clause and a dependent clause (p. 206)

Compound—two or more words, phrases, or ideas joined by a conjunction (p. 60)

Compound-complex sentence—a sentence with two or more independent clauses and one or more dependent clauses (p. 207)

Compound direct object—two or more direct objects joined by a conjunction (p. 70)

Compound object of preposition—two or more objects of one preposition joined by a conjunction (p. 56)

Compound sentence—a sentence made up of two or more complete sentences joined by a conjunction (p. 58)

Compound predicate—two or more predicates joined by a conjunction (p. 52)

Compound subject—two or more subjects joined by a conjunction (p. 52)

Compound subject complement—two or more subject complements joined by a conjunction (p. 142)

Concrete noun—a word that names something that can be seen or touched (p. 77)

Conjunction—a word that joins two or more words, phrases, or ideas in a sentence (p. 50)

Contraction—a word formed when two words are put together and letters are left out (p. 174)

D

Dependent clause—a group of words that does not form a complete thought and cannot stand alone (p. 206)

Descriptive paragraph—a paragraph that describes a person, place, or thing (p. 224)

Dialogue—conversation between two or more characters in a story (p. 231)

Direct object—a noun or pronoun that takes action directly from the verb (p. 68)

Direct quotation—the exact words that someone says (p. 210)

Double negative—the mistake of using two words that mean "no" in one sentence (p. 190)

E

Edit—checking written work for mistakes (p. 106)

Exclamation point (!)—a punctuation mark showing strong feeling (p. 4)

F

Fragment—a group of words that is not a complete sentence (p. 20)

Future tense—the tense of verbs that tells about action in the future (p. 166)

G

Greeting—word or words used before the name or title of the person to whom a letter is sent (p. 234)

H

Heading—the address of the person writing a letter (p. 234)

Helping verb—a verb that comes before the main verb. Together, the two verbs form a verb phrase (p. 160)

Homonym—a word that sounds like another word but has a different meaning and spelling (p. 244)

I

Independent clause—a complete sentence (p. 206)

Indirect object—a noun or pronoun that takes action from the verb indirectly (p. 114)

Indirect quotation—what someone says but not his or her exact words (p. 210)

Interjection—a word that shows strong feelings (p. 104)

Invitation—a written request (p. 221)

Irregular verb—a verb that changes its form to form past tenses (p. 170)

L

Lead paragraph—a paragraph that introduces a news article; it tells who, what, when, where, why, and sometimes, how (p. 222)

Linking verb—a verb that connects the subject to a word in the predicate (p. 132)

M

Memo—a clear, organized record of important facts and details (p. 220)

N

Narrative—a series of paragraphs that go together to tell a story (p. 230)

Negative—a word that means "no" or "not" that stops the action of the verb (p. 168)

Nominative pronoun—a pronoun used as the subject of a sentence (p. 78)

Noun—a word that names a person, place, or thing (p. 6)

Noun object complement—a noun that renames the direct object (p. 118)

Noun subject complement—a noun or pronoun in the predicate that renames the subject (p. 132)

O

Object complement—a word or words following the direct object that completes the meaning of the verb (p. 118)

Object of the preposition—the noun or pronoun that follows the preposition (p. 28)

Objective pronoun—a pronoun used as an object (p. 79)

Owner noun—a noun that owns something in a sentence (p. 94)

Owner pronoun—a pronoun that owns something in a sentence (p. 96)

Owner object—a noun following an owner pronoun or owner noun (p. 96)

P

Paragraph—a group of sentences about one topic (p. 224)

Past tense—the tense of verbs that tells about action in the past (p. 164)

Pattern of sentence—See Sentence pattern

Period (.)—the punctuation mark ending a sentence that makes a statement or gives a command (p. 4)

Persuasive paragraph—a paragraph that tries to make readers believe something or do something (p. 228)

Plural—more than one (p. 248)

Predicate—the part of a sentence that tells what the subject is doing (p. 4)

Preposition—a word that ties or relates a noun or pronoun to another part of the sentence (p. 28)

Prepositional phrase—a group of words that begins with a preposition and ends with a noun or pronoun (p. 28)

Present tense—the tense of verbs that tells about action in the present (p. 162)

Prewrite—talking, thinking, or reading about a topic before writing (p. 106)

Process paragraph—a paragraph that tells how something is done (p. 226)

Pronoun—a word that takes the place of a noun (p. 78)

Pronoun owner—See Owner pronoun

Proper noun—the name of a specific person, place, or thing (p. 44)

Punctuation—marks in a sentence that tell readers when to pause or stop (p. 22)

Q

Question mark (?)—a punctuation mark that ends a sentence asking a question (p. 4)

Question pronoun—a pronoun that asks (p. 204)

Quotation marks (" ")—punctuation used around the title of a part of a large work; punctuation used to begin and end a direct quotation (pp. 63, 210)

Quotation, direct—See Direct quotation

Quotation, indirect—See Indirect quotation

R

Regular verb—a verb that adds *-d* or *-ed* to form the past tense (p. 158)

Review—a writer's opinion about a movie, TV show, book, or play (p. 232)

Rewrite—writing again until the meaning is clear (p. 106)

S

Semicolon (;)—a punctuation mark that separates two related ideas not connected by a conjunction (p. 62)

Sentence—a group of words that forms a complete thought; a sentence begins with a capital letter and ends with a period, question mark, or exclamation point (p. 4)

Sentence pattern—the basic form of a sentence (p. 5)

Signature—the name signed by the writer of a letter (p. 234)

Simple predicate—one or more verbs in a sentence (p. 18)

Simple subject—one or more subject nouns or pronouns in a sentence (p. 18)

Singular—one (p. 248)

State-of-being verb—a verb that tells that the subject exists, but does not show action (p. 40)

Subject—the part of a sentence that tells who or what the sentence is about (p. 4)

Subject complement—a word in the predicate that describes the subject (p. 132)

Superlative—an adjective that compares three or more nouns (p. 152)

T

Tense—present, past, or future time expressed by a verb (p. 158)

Tone of voice—the sound of speech (p. 200)

Topic—the main idea of an essay or paragraph (p. 224)

Topic sentence—a sentence that states the main idea of a paragraph (p. 224)

U

Understood subject—a subject that cannot be seen in a sentence (p. 100)

Understood you—*you* as a subject that cannot be seen in a sentence (p. 100)

V

Verb—a word that shows action (p. 10)

Verb phrase—a verb and its helpers (p. 160)

W

Write—putting ideas on paper (p. 106)

Writing process—the use of four steps: prewrite, write, rewrite, and edit (p. 106)

Sign Alphabet

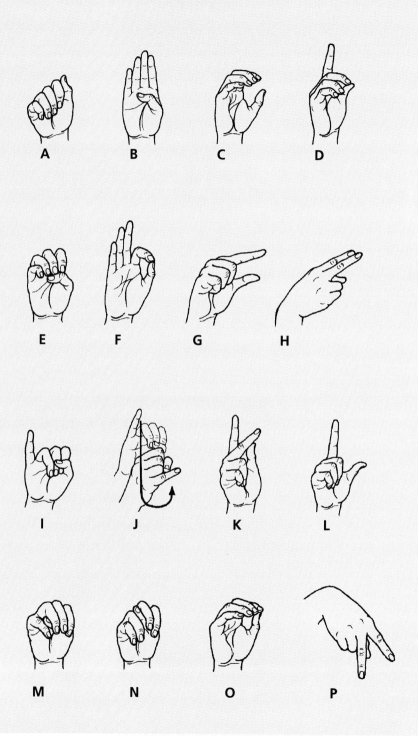

Sign Alphabet

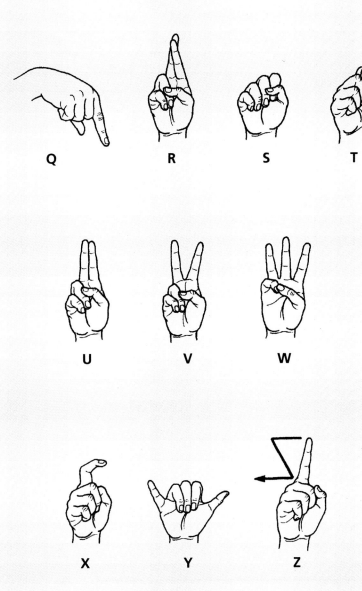

Index

A

A/an/the. See Article
Abbreviation, 194–95
Abstract noun, 77, 86, 94–95
Accept/except, 182–83
Action verb, 10–11, 68, 158
Addressing envelopes, 236
Adjective, 1, 8–9, 138–39
    adverb vs., 12–13, 140–41
    comma and, 22–23
    comparative, 152–53
    defined, 8
    pronoun vs., 82–85
    superlative, 152–53
Adjective object complement, 118–19
Adjective prepositional phrase, 30–31, 33, 38–39, 56
Adjective subject complement, 136–37
Adverb, 1, 12–17, 102–03
    adjective vs., 12–13, 140–41
    comma and, 22–23
    making comparisons, 256–57
    confusing with interjection, 105
    defined, 12
    ending in -*ly,* 13, 140–41
    preposition vs., 36–37
    questions about verb and, 12–17
Adverb prepositional phrase, 34–35, 38–40
Agreement, 262–69
    pronoun-noun, 268–69
    subject-verb, 262–67
    verb, 264–67
American Sign Language (ASL), 1
Apostrophe, 94–95, 98, 108, 174–75, 184
Appositive, 122–23, 135
    commas and, 126–27
Article *(a, an, the),* 9, 77

B

Body, 234

C

Can/may, 202–03
Capitalization, 86
Capital letter, 4, 23, 127, 194–95
    and addressing envelopes, 236
    for proper noun, 44, 63, 86–87
Clause
    dependent, 206–09
    independent, 206–07
Closing, 234
Colon, 194–95
Command, 202–03
Comma, 44–45, 87, 108, 122
    and adjective, 22–23
    and adverb, 22–23
    with appositive, 126–27
    in compound sentence, 58–59, 62–63
    with dependent clause, 208
    with interjection, 108–09, 201
    and prepositional phrase, 44–45
Common noun, 44, 77, 86, 94
Comparative, 152–53
Complement
    adjective object, 118–19
    adjective subject, 136–37
    compound subject, 142–43
    noun object, 118–19
    noun subject, 132–33
    object, 118–21
    subject, 132–33, 135, 142–45
Complete predicate, 18–19, 34, 54–55, 71
Complete sentence, 4–5, 20–21
Complete subject, 18–19, 30, 52
Complex sentence, 206–09
Compound, defined, 60
Compound-complex sentence, 207
Compound direct objects, 70–73
Compound parts, 50–63
    conjunctions and, 50–55
    in indirect objects, 116–17
    object complements and, 120–21
    prepositions and, 56–57
    punctuation and, 59, 62–63
    as sentences, 58–59, 70–73
    in sentences, 60–61
    subject complements and, 142–43
Compound predicate, 54–55
Compound sentence, 58–59, 70–73
    commas and, 59, 62–63, 87
Compound subject, 52–53, 56, 264–65
Compound subject complement, 142–43
Compound verb, 72–73
Concrete noun, 77
Conjunction, 1, 50–55, 58–59
    commonly used, 50
    defined, 50
    dependent clause, 206–09
    direct object joined by, 70–71

punctuation with, 87
Contraction, 174–75, 184–85, 190–91

D

Dependent clause, 206–09
Dependent clause conjunction, 206–07
Descriptive paragraph, 224–25
Dialogue, 231
Direct object, 68–87, 186–87
 compound, 70–73
 and nouns, 76–77
 and prepositional phrases, 74–75
 and pronouns, 78–85
 See also Adjective object complement;
 Noun object complement;
 Object complement
Direct quotation, 210–11, 214–15
Don't/doesn't, 270–71
Double negative, 190–91

E

Edit, 106–07, 172–73, 193–94, 212–13, 223–33, 276–77
Either/or, 269
English, nonstandard, 274–77
English, standard, 274–77
Envelopes, addressing, 236
Exact language, 179–95
Exclamation point, 4, 22, 108–09, 127, 200–01

F

For/to, 114–15
Fragment, 20–21
Future tense, 158–61, 166–69

G

Good/well, 13, 141, 256
Greeting, 234–35

H

Heading, 234–35
Helping verb, 160–67
Here/there, 100–01, 145, 264–65
Hidden verb. *See* State–of–being verb
Homonym, 244–47

I

-ie or -ei, 252–53
Incomplete sentence. *See* Fragment
Independent clause, 206–07
Indirect object, 114–15
 compound parts in, 116–17
Indirect quotation, 210–11
Interjection, 1, 104–05, 108–09, 201
 confusing with adverb, 105

defined, 104
 punctuation and, 108, 201
 words used as, 104
Invitation, 221
Irregular verb, 170–71
Its/it's, 184–85

J

Journal, 180–81

L

Lead paragraph, 222–23
Learn/teach, 182–83
Let/leave, 188–89
Letter
 addressing envelopes, 236
 body, 234–35
 closing, 234–35
 friendly, 234–35
 greeting, 234–35
 heading, 234–35
 signature, 234–25
Lie/lay, 186–87
Linking verb, 131–53, 158
-ly, 13, 140–41

M

Main verb, 160–61
May/can, 202–03
Memo, 220
Message, 220
Misspelled words, commonly, 242–43

N

Name of person, 86
Narrative, 230–31
Negative, 168–69
 double, 190–91
Neither/nor, 269
News story, 222–23
Nominative pronoun, 78–79, 146–47
Notes, 180–81
Not/never, 168–69
Noun, 1, 6–7, 76–77
 abstract, 77, 86, 94–95
 adjective and, 8–9
 article and, 9, 77
 common, 44, 77, 86, 94
 concrete, 77
 defined, 6
 and direct object, 76–77
 give new name, 134–35
 owner, 94–95, 98–99, 108
 plural, 248–49, 262–63

proper, 44–45, 86–87, 94
    singular, 248–49
Noun object complement, 118–19
Noun subject complement, 132–33

O

Object
    direct, 67–87, 186–87
    indirect, 114–17
    owner, 96–97
Object complement, 118–21
Objective pronoun, 79, 146
Object of preposition, 28, 32–33, 56–57
Opinion, 232–33
Owner noun, 94–95, 98–99, 108
Owner object, 96–97
Owner pronoun, 96–99, 146–47, 184–85
Ownership, 94–99, 108–09

P

Paragraph, 222–29
    descriptive, 224–25
    lead, 222–23
    persuasive, 228–29
    process, 226–27
Parts of speech, 1, 92–109
    adjective, 1, 8–9, 138–39
    adverb, 1, 12–17, 102–03
    conjunction, 1, 50–55, 58–59
    interjection, 1, 104–05, 108–09, 201
    noun, 1, 6–7, 76–77
    preposition, 1, 28–45, 56–57
    pronoun, 1, 78–85, 96–99, 146–47, 184–85
    verb, 1, 10–13, 131–53, 157–75
Past tense, 158–59, 164–65, 168–71
Pattern. See Sentence pattern
Period, 4, 22–23, 108–09, 127, 200–01
Persuasive paragraph, 228–29
Phrase
    adjective prepositional, 30–31, 33, 38–39,
        42–43, 56
    adverb prepositional, 34–43
    prepositional, 28–29, 32–33, 42–43
    verb, 160–69, 205
Plural, 248–49, 262–71
Predicate
    complete, 18–19, 34, 54–55, 71
    compound, 54–55
    in sentences, 4–5
    simple, 18–19, 34, 55
    and verb, 10, 12, 18
Preposition, 1, 28–45, 56–57
    adverb vs., 36–37

commonly used, 28
    compound, 56–57
    defined, 28
    object of, 28, 32–33, 56–57
    See also Prepositional phrase
Prepositional phrase, 28–29, 32–33, 42–43
    adjective, 30–31, 33, 38–39, 56
    adverb, 34–35, 38–40
    comma and, 44–45
    and direct object, 74–75
    and state-of-being verb, 40–41, 158
    two or more, 38–39
    See also Preposition
Present tense, 158–59, 162–63, 168–69
Prewrite, 106–07, 172–73, 192–93, 223–33
Process paragraph, 226–27
Pronoun, 1, 78–81, 146–47
    adjective and, 82–85
    defined, 78
    and direct object, 78–85
    nominative, 78–79, 146–47
    objective, 79, 146
    owner, 96–99, 146–47, 184–85
    as subject, 144–47, 266–67
    -self, 81
    using, 80–81
Pronoun-noun agreement, 268–69
Pronoun subject, 144–47, 266–67
Proofread, 212
Proper noun, 44–45, 86–87, 94
Punctuation
    apostrophe, 94–95, 98, 108, 174–75, 184
    capital letter, 4, 23, 44, 63, 86–87, 127, 194–95,
        236
    colon, 194–95
    comma, 22–23, 44–45, 58–59, 62–63, 87, 108,
        122, 126–27, 201, 208
    defined, 22
    exclamation point, 4, 22, 108–09, 127, 200–01
    period, 4, 22–23, 108–09, 127, 200–01
    question mark, 4, 22, 200–01
    quotation marks, 63, 210–11
    semicolon, 62–63, 87

Q

Question mark, 4, 22, 200–01
Question pronoun, 204–05
Questions, 202–05
Quotation
    direct, 210–11, 214–15
    indirect, 210–11
Quotation marks, 63, 210–11

R

Regular verb, 158–59, 170
Request, 202–03
Review, 232–33
Rewrite, 106–07, 172–73, 192–93, 223–33, 276–77
Rise/raise, 186–87

S

-Self pronoun, 81
Semicolon, 62–63, 87
Sentence, 1, 3–23, 199–215
    complete, 4–5, 20–21
    complex, 206–09
    compound, 58–59, 62–63, 70–73, 87
    compound-complex, 207
    fragment, 20–21
    ideas for, 150–51
    with linking verb, 131–53, 158
    meaning of, 272–73
    pattern in, 1, 5, 8, 10, 12, 14, 16, 40, 68–71, 74, 78, 100, 113–27, 142–44, 146, 148–49
    predicate of, 4–5
    subject of, 4–7
Sentence pattern, 1, 5, 8, 10, 12, 14, 16, 40, 68–71, 74, 78, 100, 113–27, 142–44, 146, 148–49
Signature, 234–35
Sign language. *See* American Sign Language
Simple predicate, 18–19, 34, 55
Simple subject, 18–19, 30, 32–33, 52–53, 56–57, 101
Singular, 248–49, 262–71
Sit, set, 186–87
Speech, parts of. *See* Parts of speech
Spelling, 182–89, 241–57
    homonym, 244–47
    -ie or -ei, 252–53
    plural, 248–49
    practice, 242–43
    similar patterns or sounds, 254–55
    singular, 248–49
    word endings, 248–51
Statement, 202–03
State-of-being verb, 40–41, 158
    commonly used, 40
    See also Linking verb
Subject
    complete, 18–19, 30, 52
    compound, 52–53, 56, 264–65
    confusing, 32–33
    hidden, 100–01
    pronoun as, 144–47
    in sentence, 4–7
    simple, 18–19, 30, 32–33, 52–53, 56–57, 101
    understood, 100–01
Subject complement, 132–33, 135, 142–45
Subject-verb agreement, 262–67
Superlative, 152–53

T

Tense
    future, 158–61, 166–69
    past, 158–59, 164–65, 168–71
    present, 158–59, 162–63, 168–69
Test Taking Tips, 25, 47, 65, 89, 111, 129, 155, 177, 197, 217, 239, 259, 279
Their/there/they're, 184–85
There/here, 100–01, 145, 264–65
These/those, 84–85
This/that, 84–85
Time, 194–95
Title
    of book, 63, 262
    of CD, 63
    of magazine, 63
    of movie, 262
    name as, 86–87
    of newspaper, 63
    of play, 262
    of poem, 262
    of song, 262
To/for, 114–15
Tone of voice, 200–01
Too/very, 102–03
Topic, 224
Topic sentence, 224–25
To/too/two, 188–89

U

Understood subject, 100–01
Understood *you,* 100–01

V

Verb, 1, 10–11, 157–75
    action, 10–11, 68, 158
    adverb and, 12–17
    compound, 72–73
    defined, 10
    helping, 160–67
    irregular, 170–71
    linking, 131–53, 158
    main, 160–61
    misused, 182–89
    regular, 158–59, 170
    state-of-being, 40–41, 158
Verb agreement, 264–67

Verb form, 162–71
Verb phrase, 160–69
Verb tense. *See* Tense
Very/too, 102–03

W

Well/good, 13, 141, 256
Word order, 5
Write, 106–07, 172–73, 192–93, 223–33
Writing mechanics, 22–23, 44–45, 62–63, 86–87,
    108–09, 126–27, 152–53, 174–75, 194–95,
    214–15, 236–37, 256–57, 276–77
    abbreviation, 194–95
    addressing envelopes, 236
    contraction, 174–75, 184–85, 190–91
    direct quotation, 210–11, 214–15
    parts of letter, 234–35
    spelling, 241–57
    See also Punctuation
Writing practice, 124–25, 150–51, 172–73,
    192–93, 212–13
Writing process, 106–07, 125, 172–73, 192–93,
    223–33
Writing skills
    paragraph, 222–29
    sentence, 1, 3–23, 199–215
    topic sentence, 224–25
    writing process, 106–07, 125, 172–73, 192–93,
        223–33
Writing, types of
    descriptive paragraph, 224–25
    dialogue, 231
    friendly letter, 234–35
    invitation, 221
    memo, 220
    message, 220
    narrative, 230–31
    news story, 222–23
    persuasive paragraph, 228–29
    process paragraph, 226–27
    request, 202–03
    review, 232–33

Y

Your/you're, 184–85